Customer Astonishment

Customer Astonishment

10 Secrets to World-Class Customer Care

by

Darby Checketts

With Foreword by Paul B. Brown
Co-Author of *Customers for Life*

Please visit www.CustomerAstonishment.com or telephone 480-654-0811.

Robert D. Reed Publishers • Bandon, OR

Robert D. Reed Publishers
P.O. Box 1992
Bandon, OR 97411
Phone: 541-347-9882 • Fax: -9883
E-mail: 4bobreed@msn.com
web site: www.rdrpublishers.com

Typesetter: **Barbara Kruger**
Cover Designer: **Grant Prescott**

ISBN 1-931741-68-9

Library of Congress Control Number 2005908467

Manufactured, typeset and printed in the United States of America

Dedication

I wish to dedicate this book to two of my client organizations that absolutely excel in their commitment to internalize and practice the principles of *Customer Astonishment*. These are: the *Customer Champions* of Ward/Kraft of Fort Scott, Kansas, and the ingenious people of Rio Salado College of Tempe, Arizona. To learn more about these fine organizations, please visit them at www.wardkraft.com and www.rio.maricopa.edu.

Acknowledgments

I give my deepest thanks to Robert Reed and Cleone Lyvonne who joined with me to envision the book and make it a reality. Thanks to Barbara Kruger and Grant Prescott for their finishing touches. The book-creation wizards of RDR Publishers have opened another door for my life's work. I also wish to acknowledge my great coach and friend, Steve Chandler, who is such a positive force for moving his clients' creativity and value-generating capabilities to the next level.

To Tom Peters, the Heart of Wow! For the past 14 years, I have researched, pondered, taught, and practiced the principles of *Customer Astonishment*. No one has contributed more to my vision of "WOW" than Tom Peters. As I prepared my clients to enter the new millennium, it was Tom's book, *The Circle of Innovation*, which truly kicked my brain doors open. As I teach *Customer Astonishment*, I begin every presentation with the idea of "You, Inc." The initial tipping point for anybody who intends to raise the bar for customer care is to embrace this Tom Peters principle...

Every-person-a-business-person, every-person-a-Michelangelo.

To Carl Sewell and Paul B. Brown for writing what I consider to be the most down-to-earth and helpful book ever written on customer care (prior to this one). I hope I have contributed to many thousands of book sales for these two gentlemen. Their book is based on the customer-focused business practices of the Sewell automobile dealerships.

To Sharon, my wife and partner, along with Myrna Lea Houston who have been my most loyal co-promoters of *Customer Astonishment*. To Harry Yoo of South Korea and Dr. Charles Cudjoe of Nigeria for their valuable international connections and partnership. To all of my clients who have become even more *astonishing*. Thank you.

Contents

Foreword
by Paul B. Brown

The only thing that separates you from the competition is the service you provide. That was true when Carl Sewell and I wrote *Customers for Life* a number of years ago; it remains true today.

Everyone has access to the same sources of capital, the same raw materials, and the same trading partners. No matter how innovative your product, it can be copied in weeks. No matter how "unique" your approach to the market, someone can figure it out and probably do it faster and cheaper.

The only way to stand out is your service. In the end, the only thing that will keep customers coming back is your service.

In the following pages, Darby has identified 10 of the key factors that will insure customers bring their business to you rather than go somewhere else. Ignore these at your peril.

– Paul B. Brown, Co-author, *Customers for Life*

* *If you're good to your customers, they'll keep coming back because they like you.*

* *If they like you, they'll spend more money.*

* *If they spend more money, you want to treat them better.*

* *And if you treat them better, they'll keep coming back and the circle starts again.*

– *Customers for Life* by Carl Sewell and Paul B. Brown

Introduction of the 10 Secrets

BOLD. Say the word. Contemplate the word. Don't be intimidated by the word. See the energy inside it. Let the energy out. Use the synonyms: daring, courageous, brave, forward thinking, and intrepid. Don't get hung up on any connotation of the word that bugs you or intimidates you. Go for the positive. Go for the energy. *This is not an age for timidity in anything.* The BOLDer the economic challenges in the world marketplace, the BOLDer companies must be to surpass these. The BOLDer the hurricanes, the BOLDer government must be to defeat their effects upon us. The more opportunity out there, the BOLDer you must be to seize it. Being timid does not serve you and it certainly does not *astonish* your customers.

What gets in the way of a BOLDer approach to growing your business and knocking the socks off your customers so that they are fiercely loyal to you? Is it a time management problem? The answer is simple: Be BOLDer. You must have the courage to say NO to your proliferating, chaotic, get-in-your-way checklists. You must stand BOLDly for true priorities. Is your excuse that you lack money for an advertising campaign? You must be BOLDer in finding new sources for the money you need. Or, you must be BOLD enough to fire your advertising agency and to get on the phone with your top 3-5 prospects and tell them you have a BOLD proposal for them that can't wait for the next ad campaign.

90% of us are masters of excuses. The other 10% are too busy moving forward to remember what the excuses may have been. There is really no good excuse for anything. Your success and happiness is not served by excuses. It is only served by the *astonishing* truth that says: *What you have learned from the past is that, STARTING TODAY, a new course of action is needed to move forward more BOLDly.* Success doesn't wait for better circumstances. Success comes to those who create better circumstances. There is a superman or a superwoman inside you.

Let him out. Let her out. Stop reading this for two minutes, grab a notepad and immediately write the three things that WILL NOW pop into your mind about which you must be BOLDer. You just recovered the investment in this book 10,000 times. Now, get ready to act with BOLDness about your business and your happiness.

While not all businesses are alike, each one can make quantum leaps forward when there is BOLD action. As we consider examples, you may not relate to some businesses that are "not like yours" and therefore fail to learn from these. Let me illustrate. I'll say one word. *Harley*. I don't even have to say *Davidson* for you to get my meaning. I remember sitting in my seat in the ballroom of the Ritz Carlton hotel in Phoenix, Arizona, listening to the vice president of one of the world's premier hotel chains. He was conducting a discussion about examples of superlative customer loyalty. Various ideas were kicked round. Finally, and I was there (didn't read this in a magazine), I heard a vice president of Harley-Davidson stand up and say what must have now been quoted a zillion times, but please hear it again. He said, "I'd like to propose that the ultimate manifestation of customer loyalty is when your customers tattoo your company logo on their bodies." Wow! Top that!

Eat your heart out Hewlett-Packard—another great (two-name, hyphenated) American company. I have been fiercely loyal to HP laser printers for years. As with most companies, the folks at HP continually face new challenges to reinvent themselves. Perhaps they haven't reached the pinnacle until computer aficionados tattoo "HP" on their chests or upper arms. Now, remember what I said about not discounting an idea because you don't relate to it. I am not advocating tattoos. I am making a point. Learn from it. Harley-Davidson has created pure magic for their customers. I dare to say that, of those American males who don't already own one, 74% fantasize about owning a Harley and the other 26% hide the truth. Plenty of American females have a Harley fetish as well. Work to understand the Harley magic and apply it to your business—even if you're selling laser printers or family scrapbooks. How can you create a Harley experience for your customers?

In this book, we'll talk about many great companies, large and small. We'll talk about having a Core Purpose for your business and an intense Customer Focus. But, before we lay the bricks and mortar (the 10 Secrets and more), let's talk about Starbucks. I'm not just on the bandwagon here promoting Starbucks. I'm learning from them. I want you to recognize the cult-like symbolism of folks walking around the airport or shopping mall with their Starbucks cups, with those famous brown cardboard "holder thingees." Here's the magic of Starbucks. They transcend everything non-BOLD about selling coffee, hot chocolate, designer fruit juices, and more. Their mission is to provide a REFUGE for their customers. Read that again. They aren't just selling coffee or the hot chocolate I love so much or pastries or coffee beans and coffee makers. All these are available in the store to create revenue for Starbucks as you find REFUGE. Refuge from what? *From ordinariness. From your boss. From the noise of the world and the traffic outside. From the cold weather and air pollution. From some of your frantic family members. From your otherwise sense that the world has just come to an end because your company is shutting down your divisional office.*

Once you have that warm "cuppa" in your hand and settle down in that nice, friendly wooden chair to soak in that earthy green motif, the world comes into focus. Soon, you will be ready to face your boss, brave the weather, and call your frantic family member to reassure them that your office closure doesn't mean the family is about to be homeless. Thanks Starbucks.

What can you REALLY do for your customers? Where can you BREAK OUT from your timid thinking? What did you learn from this introduction to *Customer Astonishment*? It is one thing: BOLD. This book will guide you act BOLDly to positively *astonish* your customers, including the creation of a "culture of service excellence" that will mean *Customer Astonishment* has become part of your organizational DNA. *Customer Astonishment* begins with you, emanates from your team, and grabs your customers with the idea that somebody really cares about what they need and want. They don't want ordinary. They may not want extreme. Or, they may want extreme. For sure they want to be served by those who think and act BOLDly to help solve their problems and make life better, more satisfying, more exciting, more meaningful, and a *more powerful experience for them*. And, who, in the end, will be served and *astonished* most of all? You will!

Park your Harley. Grab a Starbucks. Read on.

Or, should I say, *rock on*—with BOLDness.

Preview: 10 Secrets to World-Class Customer Care

#1: Be Customer Champions! Know what your team *stands for* and communicate it through words and actions. Champion your *core purpose* in direct response to what your customers want and need most.

#2: Get Connected. Know the interdependencies represented by your own *Chain of Customers*. Make communication *linkage* a top priority that demonstrates the importance of all of your customers, internal and external.

#3: Get It Together. Quickly resolve internal conflicts so these do not become apparent and weaken the customer's confidence in your team. Achieve crystal clear agreement on team priorities and individual responsibilities.

#4: Know Your Customers. Listen to them. Observe them. The commitment is to NO SURPRISES, except on their birthdays. What you promise is what they get and more.

#5: Know the Bear. There is a bear out there, behind you. Faster is not fast enough. Reliable is not reliable enough. World Class means you set a standard for the world to follow. The bear cannot keep up.

#6: Take Ownership. Champion the idea that "I am the one." For each member of your team, this means, "I am the one who first spoke with the customer. And, at the end of the day, I am the one who will follow through to be sure WE met the customer's needs."

#7: Stake Your Reputation. Create your very own *Hallmarks of Professional Excellence*. Seize those crucial *moments of truth* in a way that shows your true commitment to each customer.

#8: Add Value at Each Step of the Way. Be sure that whatever it is that you do, you do it with the customer in mind.

#9: Smooth the Way. Always treat the customer as an honored guest. Never place your convenience above that of the customer. Your professionalism will shine as you do.

#10: Create Options. Don't say "No" to the customer. NO is often uncreative. YES is great, but may be over-commitment. The customer needs options. Create these. Even partial solutions are better than roadblocks. Be a world-class problem solver!

Author's Special Note

The first five chapters of this book are about PREPARATION. Use these chapters to *fuel the fire* and *start your creative engines*. As you do, you will also set the stage for the specific *Customer Astonishment* principles and methods to follow.

...Chapter 1 will enlighten you.
...Chapter 2 will challenge you to sweep the floors, take out the trash, and mow the lawn.
...Chapter 3 will challenge you to raise the bar.
...Chapter 4 will put you in the driver's seat.
...Chapter 5 will provide a powerful, four-dimensional strategy to guide you.

Then, the *10 Secrets* will constitute the second section of the book. One by one, these will guide you to intensify your customer commitments to ensure that every dimension of your business strategy and every aspect of your interaction with customers are *world-class*.

Read each chapter with a highlighter in hand to capture your own favorite points. Make note of any key principles you especially want to remember along with those specific ideas that occur to you that will directly benefit your customers. As you read, consider the *Be-Do-Achieve* of personal leadership: what you intend to *Achieve*, based on the things you must *Do*, powered by who you must *Be* to succeed.

We have entered an especially dynamic age of business. Gary Hamel, author of *Leading the Revolution*, stated, "You can't use an old map to find a new land." In his newest revolutionary book, *Re-Imagine*, Tom Peters challenges us to re-imagine the world. He emphasizes that *real excellence is always a moving target*.

This book will help you find the target. It is your new map to greater customer loyalty and a dramatic boost in your business success. As you place a renewed emphasis on world-class customer care, employee morale will be strengthened, productivity will increase, your financial performance will improve, and your business will grow. What's more, you will achieve your personal goals and prosper. *As with any reliable map, this book is here to guide you, but it's up to you to plot the course, set the sails, and steer the ship.*

In the pages that follow, you will learn from many examples of real-world organizations. Some of these organizations are unimaginative and failing. I will not use their names, but I will remain hopeful that they will learn from their mistakes. Some companies may have been acquired or re-organized by the time you read the book. Learn from the evolution that brings about such changes. Some of my examples of *excellence* are situational. The organization itself may be imperfect, but you will learn from the good they do and the progress they're making. For instance, every time I write about Apple Computer I have to either *hold my breath* or *catch my breath*. What excitement they create. When they make a mistake, it hits the headlines. When they succeed, it hits the headlines. But, they always LEAD. They always re-imagine the map. Some of my examples are timeless. Other examples of excellence will be leapfrogged by tomorrow morning. Begin to scan for your own examples of those organizations and individuals that are truly *astonishing*. Then, be the leapfrog. Be BOLD. Be BOLDer yet!

Section I: Get Ready

Chapter 1
Rock the World

Let's begin a quest for *Customer Astonishment* and those organizations that rock the world for their customers. Yours will be one of them. As we conclude this chapter, we will consolidate our definitions of key words and concepts.

Customer Astonishment is the result of pure genius, outrageous creativity, exceptional diligence, daring to be different, amazing consistency, a little extra work, and/or some genuine thoughtfulness. It will always be BOLD because it somehow breaks from the ordinary and from timidity. It may light up the sky with fireworks. It may warm the heart. It may cause a sigh of contentment, a chuckle of relief, a profound thank you, or a right out loud "wow." It may require a serious investment or it may be absolutely easy to do and inexpensive as well. It will always produce a return on your investment that far outweighs any cost. How can you be sure? Your customers will come back for more *and* bring their friends.

Harley-Davidson Softail

To illustrate that a Harley is more than just a "macho machine," let me tell you about a friend who owns a variety of motorcycles. One is for off-road fun, another is for the quick trip to his office, and one is a foreign-bred collector's item. His stable of motorcycles does include a top-of-the-line, classic Harley, which he seldom rides. I asked him why he bought it…what it's for. He replied, "When I'm bored on a Sunday afternoon, I go out in the garage, sit on the floor and look at it." Initially, I thought his motorcycles were about zoom-zoom transportation. My friend reminded me that some of these are also sculpture that brings *joy to the eye of the beholder*. And, people often pay far more for sculpture than they do for transportation. *Customer Astonishment is about exquisite product design.*

Southwest Airlines

I was once waiting at the gate in Omaha, Nebraska, or Des Moines, Iowa, for a Southwest Airlines flight. I can't remember the airport, but I will never forget the experience. The Southwest agent came to the gate and announced that there would be a 20-30 minute delay while their mechanics made a minor repair to the aircraft to assure our safety. I always appreciate concern for my safety, but I was anxious to get home and disappointed, as were the other passengers, I'm sure. Then, just as I was readjusting my expectations, the Southwest agent announced a contest. She said, "To help the wait go quickly, I'm going to conduct a simple 'hole in the sock' contest. We're going to give a $100 travel coupon to whichever one of you in the waiting area has the biggest hole in his or her sock." There was immediate laughter. The kids in the waiting area began ripping off their Nikes and waving a wide variety of holey socks in the air. Women carefully checked for qualifying runs in their nylons. We middle-aged guys in suits did a dignified peek at our socks as we slipped the loafers off the backs of our heels. Soon, one businessman jumped up, stuck his foot in the air and said, "Bet you can't beat that." The whole heel of his sock was blown out. He won. *Customer Astonishment is about raw creativity and a dead-on sense of humor.* And, in what seemed an instant, we were boarding our flight.

McCormick and Schmick's Seafood Restaurant

Last Friday was my wife's birthday. I called McCormick's on Camelback Road in Phoenix for reservations. The woman on the phone asked, "Is this a special occasion?" I answered, "Yes." The conversation continued. *May I ask the occasion?* It's my wife's birthday. *And, what is her name, if I may ask?* Sharon. *Thank you very much.* I figured Sharon would be in for a free piece of cake with a little candle and perhaps a serenade. When we got to the restaurant, sat down, and were handed our menus, there at the top of the fresh seafood and house specialties menu were the BOLD words: **Happy Birthday Sharon**. *Customer Astonishment is about forethought based on knowing just a little something special about each customer.*

Arizona Department of Transportation – Motor Vehicle Division

Our Arizona DOT Motor Vehicles Department seems to be constantly under fire from those who must renew licenses of many kinds. The lines and the wait are never short enough. Nevertheless, I know they work to find breakthroughs in the face of the challenging circumstances faced by so many government agencies. What I'll never forget is when our son, Matt, went to get his Arizona driver's license at the landmark age of 16. He returned with his shiny new card. I examined it, turned it over, and was *astonished* to see the expiration date as his 65th birthday. *Customer Astonishment is about eliminating the odious impact of bureaucracy on tax-paying citizens.* Thanks to the creative folks at the MVD, Matt would spend very few hours of his life standing in lines to get his driver's license renewed. And, there was an underlying incentive to maintain a good driving record to guarantee this preferred status, which his parents appreciated. I know this MVD program has recent variations based on various driver qualifications, but my son will be grateful for many years to come.

I recently had my driver's license renewal deadline extended five years without a visit to the MVD offices. If I remember, I think I paid four bucks online and the updated license came in the mail. That's no line and no wait. That's progress. Sometimes, we've got to give an organization a break for trying real hard to push the envelope wherever they can.

Trustworthy Services

Isn't it great when a company lives up to its name? Terry and Calvin have serviced our air conditioners for years and their consistent quality of service resulted in their winning the opportunity to install two brand new units this spring. We are always impressed with the simple commitment of these two gentlemen to putting those disposable blue booties over their work shoes before entering our home. The *astonishing* thing here isn't the concern for keeping our carpet clean. We expect that. It is the *absolute consistency* of this behavior, which is a one of several habitual manifestations of their overall courtesy and respect for us as their customers. The bottom line for these two gentlemen is: When they're at our home providing service, *Terry and Calvin never put their convenience above ours as their customers.* That's what *Customer Astonishment* is about.

Holiday Inn – Yuma, Arizona

And here's the finale to this chapter with my favorite story for painting the overall picture of *what Customer Astonishment is truly ALL about.*

The hotel conference room was full. People had traveled from several cities in and around Arizona for a public seminar in late August. As I concluded my introduction to the concept of *Customer Astonishment*, one gentleman from San Diego, California, enthusiastically raised his hand to offer his most recent "*astonishing* encounter." I will let him tell the story of his drive to Phoenix through the bustling city of Yuma, Arizona…

> *As I traveled from my home in San Diego, I had intended to drive straight through to Phoenix. However, it was early evening and I was getting a little hungry and somewhat tired. I was also having a hard time seeing out of my windshield as it had become covered with more bugs and grasshoppers than I had ever encountered anywhere. I was entering Yuma, Arizona, and I began to wonder just what they grow on the numerous farms in the surrounding area. I*

later learned that they grow citrus, cotton, onions, lettuce and many other crops. I decided to stay in Yuma for the night, so I began to look for a hotel. Just ahead, I saw the Holiday Inn with its familiar green sign. I pulled in, parked, went to the office, and was given my room assignment and hotel room keys. I walked upstairs and into my room and placed my suitcase on the bed. Then, as I usually do, I quickly surveyed the room, looking for the TV remote and the luggage stand inside the closet and double checking for decent towels and some shampoo in the bathroom.

My stomach started to growl and I realized I should go to a gas station before it got too late to clean my windshield. If I waited until morning, I would find a caked-on mess of dead bugs. I called the hotel office and asked for the location of the nearest Circle K. I then walked out onto the front balcony to head down the stairs to my car. I saw my car just below. Standing next to it was a young teenager with a bucket of sudsy stuff and a squeegee carefully cleaning my windshield. **I was astonished.** *I would never have expected a moderately priced hotel in a smaller town in southwestern Arizona to clean my windshield. They stopped cleaning windshields at gas stations 20 years ago. And, I had stayed at four-star hotels in Phoenix, paid 10 bucks to park my car, and they never cleaned my windshield. Wow! I knew where I would stay the next time I was in Yuma and it had nothing to do with TV remotes, luggage stands, shampoo or towels. These, I expected. But that one simple act of saving me the trouble of cleaning my windshield will bring me back.*

Customer Astonishment: The Path to Customer Loyalty

Here is the major message: By providing my seminar friend the commodities he expected in his hotel room, the Holiday Inn had serviced his needs. By one simple anticipatory act of cleaning his windshield, *they had serviced his loyalty.*

You may imagine that *Customer Astonishment* is some grandiose or radically cool act intended to "blow the customer's mind." Some even fear that *Customer Astonishment* may cost a lot of money. Grandiose may be okay if you're entertaining the Queen of England. Radically cool may be radically cool. But, *Customer Astonishment* is usually not complicated or expensive. It is any act or added value that is beyond what the customer expects; that represents thinking AHEAD for the customer and thinking BEYOND your competition. By cleaning the bugs from my seminar friend's windshield, the hotel had "smoothed the way" for his journey the next morning. He expected the hotel to contribute to a good night's rest. He did not expect that they would help his automobile journey be less bothersome by eliminating the need for a tired business man to go to the Circle K in his nice wool slacks and maneuver a squeegee to remove bugs.

Where do you think the Holiday Inn came up with such an idea? They had probably been competing with La Quinta, the Comfort Inn, and other nearby hotels. After a while, the price wars had become meaningless. The "loyalty factor" is not about saving a few dollars on a hotel room or even about nice bedspreads or ample designer shampoo in the bathroom. Someone at the front desk had undoubtedly noticed that every third customer who came in during the late summer months was asking directions to the convenience store or a gas station to clean their windshields. The front desk clerk had shared this observation with the manager who realized that the young person who mowed the lawn and swept the driveway often had some downtime and could, at the end of the day, clean a few windshields. The cost was minimal. The Holiday Inn immediately distinguished itself from the competition. And, the result was *astonishing*.

Beyond Customer Service...Beyond Customer Satisfaction

Customer Astonishment goes beyond traditional customer service. *Customer service* is merely an activity. To service something or to give service to someone is to perform an activity or a set of procedures required by the customer to meet a need or to satisfy some desire. Such performance might be perfunctory and perhaps just meet the *minimum* requirement.

This book will challenge you to move beyond an "activity focus" to a "results focus." *Customer satisfaction* is the *result* of customer service activities performed well. Service is the performance. Satisfaction is the result. To perform without the desired result is merely "to go through the motions." What's more, in today's highly competitive world, *even customer satisfaction is no longer enough.* Why? The answer: because a "satisfied" customer is still shopping around. To illustrate: Suppose you visit a new restaurant and as you leave there is a reporter from the local television station standing outside to ask you how you liked The Yangtze River Diner. You reply, "The food was good. Yes, they took care of us. It's a nice restaurant." Quite frankly, this is the language of diners who never go back. If you are the restaurant owner, the words you hope the television reporter hears are, "Oh, ooh, oh my, their Moo Shu Chicken is to die for. I can't begin to describe their service. You'll have to go and see for yourself. Wow!" These customers are coming back and bringing their friends soon.

Definition: To Strike with Awe and Wonder

My commitment is to support you and your organization as you move beyond traditional customer service to this new age of *Customer Astonishment.* And, here is the definition of the powerful word *astonish.* To *astonish* is "to strike with awe and wonder." This is not to be confused with the word *astound* which means "to shock and bewilder." If you astound your customers, you may lose them. And, by the way, *to serve* is merely to "satisfy the requirements of," which is not enough. The message for each of us is simply this: *how you and I view those we serve is at the heart of who we are professionally and how successful we will become.* In other words, you must be *competent* and you must *care* enough to do your very best.

Together, we will explore the secrets I have been working to uncover and which our many Cornerstone clients have helped to identify and crystallize for you. Some of these are breakthrough ideas. Some are timeless truths in modern clothing. Whether you are a dentist, a restaurant operator, a corporate vice president, a schoolteacher, a social worker, a heavy equipment operator, a bank teller, a computer programmer, a movie star, or a United States Senator, you are in business...the business of life and the business of delivering a product or a service that others depend on. They may not always give you the recognition you deserve, but they know the difference between those who care about what they do and the people they serve, and those who don't. If you're reading this book, you care about your customers. You are a professional. You are ready to be BOLD. Let's raise the bar. Let's rock the world of your customers. Read on.

Chapter 2

Beware Bloopers, Blunders, or Worse

As we proceed down the *Customer Astonishment* path to Customer Loyalty and discover the 10 Secrets to World-Class Customer Care, we need to first clear the path of the rocks and debris, and prepare to pave the way.

I caution my clients about the existence of **DLTWID**s, the *Dumb Little Things We Innocently Do* that annoy our customers. Of greater concern are **GHOST**s, those *Gaping Holes Or Serious Traps* that will derail customer relationships. So, let's clear the path. Here are some examples of customer care gone wrong—customer care bloopers or worse. Please notice: in this book, I will name names when individuals or organizations do well or when they are striving for excellence. When there are screw-ups, I will give no names to protect the negligent. However, I hope that those who read the book, who are guilty, will take note, especially when they are being blind-sided by something that can easily be fixed. And, once fixed, their performance will be much more consistent with who they intend to be and what their organizations stand for. I also realize that some of these examples are "situational" and not necessarily typical of the individuals and organizations represented. These folks undoubtedly do much better when their eyes are open and they try harder.

Cap Flap, Cap Flop

There is a hair styling gel I really like. I can only buy it at the hairstylist's salon. I use it every day. It works very well. In fact, it works better than any brand I've ever tried, but then... About halfway through the tube of gel, they really tick me off. If I didn't love the stuff, I'd stop buying it. So, why do they do this thing to me that ticks me off? Why not fix this DLTWID that gets in the way of an otherwise perfect relationship? What is the problem? The plastic flip-top hinges on the tube cap break and I must resort to unscrewing the main cap from then on, as I finish the remainder of the product. This has happened a dozen times. It's so predictable that I begin to chuckle half way through each tube knowing I'm about to get zapped. Please. Fix it. Fix it. Fix it. Whatever you're saving on the cheap little flip-top plastic hinges, it's not worth it. Your reputation gets tarnished every time it breaks. You're being "cheap." It's a flop. It's a DLTWID.

There's a Pony Somewhere.

Brace yourself, medical professionals. Hopefully, you'll find this next story hard to believe, but please accept that it's true. I have a very special family friend who recently had laser eye surgery. Yikes. Such a procedure would create anxiety for any of us. Not long after the surgery, the lens became partially detached and her vision blurred. Her doctor has been working faithfully with her to resolve the situation. Friends have been praying for her. She has been trying to be patient and have faith that all will be well. On a recent visit, the doctor tried to reassure her by saying, "Well, even if we can't clear up the blurriness in your right eye, you can still qualify for a driver's license with just one eye."

Now, some of you are picking yourselves up off the floor in disbelief. A few of you may be so optimistic that you're happy about the driver's license and missed the point. You're like the little boy, in the familiar joke, who finds horsy droppings and is delighted because it must mean there's a pony somewhere nearby. Perhaps my friend's eye is permanently injured and the doctor has done all he can do. So, what's the problem? Answer: total insensitivity in the doctor's phraseology. I realize that most doctors don't attend as many communication skills seminars as you and I do, but come on. My friend is deeply concerned that she is going blind in one eye. It is little consolation that she can still get a driver's license. She is an optimist, by the way, but right now she's a scared optimist.

I'd Love Your Business; I Just Don't Want It.

A few months ago, Sharon and I decided to diversify our sources of financial advice. A very pleasant and intelligent young man who operated a neighborhood financial services store happened to knock on our door one day. We decided to give him a try. We made an initial appointment for him to come to our home at 7:00 p.m. in the evening. We arranged our evening and waited patiently as it became 7:15, 7:20, etc. Finally, we called his cell phone. He said he was at his office as he thought that's where the meeting was supposed to be. (Note: He had not called us.) He apologized and said he'd be right over. He came. We talked. We then set our next appointment as a noontime visit to his office, which would be during a business lunch break for both Sharon and me. Our soon-to-be new financial advisor asked us to complete a couple of forms and to drop these off at his office the following day.

When I stopped at his office the next morning, the receptionist indicated that something had come up with our next appointment and that it needed to be rescheduled. The young man heard my voice and stepped out of his office to greet me. He invited me into his office to negotiate a new, mutually convenient time. I asked about a 5:00 p.m., end of the workday time slot. He said that he always tried to leave the office at that time to be home for dinner with his family. Then, I asked about a Tuesday evening appointment. He indicated that on Tuesdays he was involved with the Boy Scouts (an organization which I wholeheartedly support). I asked about a Thursday, mid-afternoon. He indicated that he had to leave early that day for his kids' soccer practice (or was it baseball?). Finally, I gave up. I thanked him for his time (of which he obviously had very little to spend with me) and asked his assistant for my paperwork as I left the office never to return.

What's the message? Family dinners are a priority. Boy Scouts make the world a better place. Kids' soccer practices are important. But, these are HIS problems not mine. This fellow's whole litany said to me, "Mr. Potential New Customer, you are my second priority. I would like to help you, but I actually have enough business to meet my needs. I prefer to work just six hours a day so that I have time for all the other stuff I love to do more than to serve you." I'm still puzzled as to why he bothered to make a sales call to our home in the first place. Among the words I said to him as I left the office were these, "Congratulations, you are obviously a very successful young man and so fortunate to already have all the business you need."

What's the BIG message: **If you're in business, you're in business. Be there.** If you'd rather not be in business, go home. And, when you're home, really be there. Soak it up. Love your family. Then, when you return to the office, really be there. Put the customer on a pedestal. Rather than share all the busy stuff on your calendar that makes it inconvenient for you to meet with the customer, give the customer three calendar options and wait for the response. If the customer can fit one of these options into his or her schedule, make the commitment and keep it.

Swamped in the Pool Store

Not long ago, I stood in a swimming pool supply store where there was a single sales clerk on duty. There were three customers in the store. The first customer was having great difficulty getting her credit card to work in the countertop credit card machine. I was there to have my pool water tested and buy a few products to correct a problem with yellow algae. So, the clerk was quite busy with one hand on the credit card gizmo and the other holding a vial containing my pool water. The credit card fiddling went on. The water testing went on. The third customer in the store was walking up and down the aisles looking at stuff and waiting for the two-ring circus at the front counter to conclude. It didn't. He left. As he did, the sales clerk looked at me and said, "Good. I'm glad he left."

Now, bless this poor fellow's heart, he was swamped—there all alone in the pool store. What's the message? Rule #1: We all know to at least acknowledge the third customer somehow or do we?

Rule #2: Don't say you're glad a customer just left while looking into the eyes of another customer. Rule #3: For the pool store manager, be aware of the work environment you've created. Is the credit card machine broken and in need of replacement? Is the store staffing level adequate? Have your employees had some very basic training in what it means to run a business? *It is amazing to me how one of the scariest GHOSTs out there is that so many front-line employees do not consider themselves to be "in business." Too often, the insight and the incentives are missing.*

Clued-In or Clueless?

The bottom line of this chapter is not to provide a venting exercise for me or for you. We all have numerous customer service horror stories. And, yes, we will continue to examine some don'ts along with the do's to further contrast World-Class customer care with customer care failure. The purpose of this chapter is to encourage you to do some initial self-examination as a business professional. Stand back from your operation and answer these straightforward questions...

1. What messages do we unintentionally send customers that are inconsistent with how important these customers are? (Under Secret #1, we will further examine: "Just who are your customers and how important are they?")

2. What obstacles may be in the way—the rocks and debris—that need to be eliminated or smoothed out to pave the way for Customer Loyalty?

3. Do we put customers on a pedestal or not? How? How not?

4. Do we have the skill and the presence of mind to deal with all the other stuff going on in our business (and in our lives) so that we're not distracted from putting them on the pedestal?

5. Do we really want to succeed by making customer relationships a priority or are we pretending that enough business will walk through the door that we can afford to "blow off" a customer here and there?

6. What little annoyance have we ignored for too long that just needs to be fixed now? Do we recognize the little things that are really big things to many customers?

7. Do we pay attention to the work environment to head off those situations that say, "Our employees are just clerks, not business people"? (Watch for Secret #2, coming soon in a book near you.)

8. Where have we left the door open for our competition or for unflattering and damaging scrutiny of some kind?

9. Where is our reputation at stake? Where are we weak and not BOLD enough?

I remember when we started our business 20 years ago. I remember praying for just one customer—tall, short, pleasant, rude, good-looking or homely—it didn't matter. We just needed someone to whom we could send an invoice. If you don't love customers, you have probably never started your own business or worked on straight commission. When you do, you realize that great customer relationships make the world go around. Customers give us the opportunity to apply our talents to serve them. Then, they let us transfer money from their bank accounts to ours so that we have the financial leverage to achieve our goals. This simple, everyday economic interdependence is what business success, professional accountability, and personal prosperity are all about. You cannot afford bloopers, blunders, DLTWIDs, or GHOSTs. Start your quest for *Customer Astonishment* by eliminating these.

Chapter 3
Top of the Mind

Let's begin with the outcome in mind. The intended outcome is that your brand will sit squarely at the *tops of the minds* of your customers, key prospects, and others who will be joining them. The vision will be to create distinctive products and services. This is the moment when you decide where you want to set the standards for your performance—standards that will make an unforgettably positive impression on your customers. You will distinguish your business from that of your competitors. Then, you will *personally* prepare to lead your team as you implement the *10 Secrets to World-Class Customer Care* that will make this outcome, vision, and distinctive reputation a reality.

Ultimately, your brand will be right there at the "top of the mind" of each person who can benefit from what you and your associates do so well. You will be somehow different from "all the others." Yes, the goal is to DISTINGUISH yourselves, to provide products that are DISTINCTIVE, and to be DIFFERENT from all the others. There is no more important preoccupation at this moment than to determine what will make you extraordinary, to stand out from the confusion of the "mass market" in a noisy world. You want customers to SEE you, to really HEAR your brand name, and to easily remember YOU because you are at the TOPS of THEIR MINDS.

Amazon, Lexus, and J-Lo

Who comes to the top of your mind when I say *Get Books*? **Amazon.com**. Who comes to the top of your mind when I say *Luxury Japanese Automobile*? **Lexus**. Who comes to the top of your mind when I say *Talented, Attractive Hispanic Actress*? **Jennifer Lopez**. What comes to the top of your mind when I say *Blow Your Nose*? **Kleenex**. Who comes to mind when I say *Golf*? **Tiger Woods**. Who comes to mind when I say *Overnight Delivery*? **FedEx**. Who comes to mind when I say *Take Care of the Poor*? **Mother Teresa**. Who comes to mind when I say *Your Favorite High School Teacher*? _____? Who comes to mind when I say *Someone You Trust to Shampoo Your Carpets*? _____? Now, we've gone from global to local. Your favorite high school teacher and who you trust to shampoo your carpets are up-close-and-personal choices. What these all have in common is that these individuals and organizations own or nearly own a category of products or services and have won a place at the *top of your mind* as being at the *top of their industry* or the *top of their game*. What category are you working on? When does your name or your brand come to the *tops of the minds* of those who are important to you in business?

How did these individuals and organizations get where they are? What would it take for you to gain "Top of the Mind" recognition in your marketplace, with your customers—to be distinguished, distinctive, and different from all the others? If you are part of a large company with a regional, national, or global presence, what will it take to get your *brand* more into the minds and into the hearts of those you wish to reach? I have recently noticed one very large and yet relatively quiet company, **BASF**, running ads to wake us up and put their company on our radar screens, nearer the top of our minds. They tell us that we may not know their company name, but we use products that they enhance for our benefit. **BASF** is working to move higher in our collective consciousness, toward the top of our minds.

When it comes to local excellence, I've already told you who comes to the top of my mind for air conditioner products and services: **Trustworthy Services**. Where do you stand as a professional, as a small locally-owned business, or as a vital organization within a larger corporation, or as a government agency, community college, or other institution? Does your name come to the top of the minds of those you serve and intend to serve? If not, what's getting in the way?

Upset of the Century

As you contemplate these questions, you are beginning the process of setting goals for your business, for raising the bar, for redefining what you stand for, for rethinking your value proposition, so you can be different from all the others. As you do, let me invite you to learn from one of the greatest "top of the mind" upsets of all time. For many years, I would talk about Sony Corporation's ownership of the category of "personal, portable entertainment." Decades ago, they made the quantum leap from bookshelf boom boxes to the Sony Walkman. At the moment they launched the Walkman, they took ownership of the category and their brand names became household words. In just the past two years, Sony's decades of leadership have been overturned by a saucy, incredibly creative American company. They have rightfully "stolen" Sony's cherished "top of the mind" position.

What is not to love about Apple? I've loved them through their high profile, struggling for survival, and phenomenally successful years. Why? ...BECAUSE THEY ARE ALWAYS DIFFERENT SOMEHOW, and I am absolutely *astonished* by their perpetual creativity and energy. I also love Sony, but the iPod is Sony's worst nightmare. Study this product. Study this company. Study Apple. And, study Sony. Watch them recover and go after Apple as they should. You don't have to be a Wall Street analyst. Read the literature. Trust what you intuitively know about each company. Where did the great Sony miss a beat (or two)? What did they overlook? Where does Apple get it right? Examine specifically what Apple has done historically...has repeatedly done over the years...and continues to do that allows them to go boom, zoom, survive getting beaten back, and then return to bust open new markets and lead the way. I know of no other company that has such an uncanny ability to resurrect itself and then take the world by a storm. With the family of iPod products, they may have finally made their ultimate mark upon the world. No, that's silly. Who could possibly know what Apple is secretly dreaming up for 2010? The iPod will yield to some new Apple (and/or Pixar) wonder, you can bet. Their new momentum is unstoppable.

So what is Apple's secret? Not long ago, *Fortune Magazine* named Apple the "World's Hottest Company." If you haven't been to an Apple retail store, go soon. Feel the creative energy in the place. Do you dare to be as creative as Apple? Do you have the staying power to get you through the challenging times BECAUSE your customers stay fiercely loyal to you always and forever? (Read: Macintosh lovers.) Is your logo as cool and as simple as Apple's? And, what is your iPod breakthrough product or service that will distinguish you and give you that "top of the mind" recognition you crave? Have I put Apple at the top of your mind as a team to watch, to admire, and to learn from? Can your company emulate Apple? No, don't. Then, you'd be the same as Apple. Learn from Apple and be different.

Today, the Neighborhood; Tomorrow the World

Here's some excellent advice. One of my mentors once told me that too many professionals and smaller businesses attempt to conquer the world before they conquer their own back yard. Your top-of-the-mind recognition begins with your local marketplace and with your already-loyal customers who will help you create the word of mouth that will make you grow, grow some more, and then find yourself ready to conquer the world.

This book is not about writing business plans or obtaining funds for business expansion, nor is it a marketing guide. Its purpose is to prepare you to do such an *astonishing* job of winning the commitment of your team members and the loyalty of your customers that this loyalty becomes the bedrock foundation upon which you build your so-called *business enterprise*. Your solid base of customers and their brand loyalty will be the platform from which you leverage the future. The challenge for you at this moment is to set your sights on the future. Get your team together.

Answer the following 21 questions to stimulate your creativity and start the engines.

Power Up / Creativity On

1. **Be Different.** How will you be different? How will you be different from all the others so that your customers SEE you in the crowd, HEAR you above all the noise, and REMEMBER you above all the others, so that you will come to the top of their minds often and whenever they need you or their friends need you? This is the BIG, very BIG question that should be at the top of your mind.

2. **Reinvent.** What is the greatest potential factor for causing what you currently sell or do to become obsolete? Get over it. Get past it. What will you do to reinvent your product line, your business, yourselves?

3. **Think Global.** What foreign country clearly needs or would be intrigued with your product or service? Why? As such expansion makes sense or as you dare to cross the oceans or venture beyond your borders, what international leverage will you seek?

4. **Join Forces.** If your product is a standardized commodity, with what other product or service could it be "embedded" or included? What is your head start on such a partnership?

5. **Retire a Cash Cow.** Which of your "cash cows" should you retire early so that it doesn't blind-side you and distract you from investing in the next generation of products and services?

6. **Govern BOLDly.** If you are a government agency and were to be privatized, how would the new organization look and perform differently? Act like an efficient government. Think like Apple.

7. **Set the Standard.** What is it about your organization that makes your competition worry? What makes them laugh? How can you intensify their worries and silence the laughter? It's

okay to be competitive. Nike is. FedEx is. Tiger Woods is. Focus your energy on beating "your previous best," not on beating *them*. What standard will you set that will become *the product/service standard* to beat in your industry?

8. **Be a Household Word.** How could your product become a product for every person—a household item such as Kleenex? What's your plan to conquer the neighborhood and then the world? [In our neighborhood, there's a restaurant that is the restaurant to beat. It is **Red, White, and Brew: Bold American Dining.** I love that 5th word. Sharon and I are fiercely loyal.]

9. **Create Surprising Alliances.** What business alliance would represent the most surprising partnership for you? Why surprising? Because others may whisper: Why would *Joe's Dry Cleaners* partner with *Red, White, and Brew*? Would the alliance be surprising or surprisingly powerful? What is your plan to approach this potential partner?

10. **Change Now.** If your most important customer acquired you, what would they change? Change it now.

11. **Be Far Out.** What is the most far out, nearly unbelievable new direction you could create for your organization? What is the first step in that direction? When, *today*, will you take it?

12. **Stop Fear.** What are you afraid of or reluctant to do and perhaps need to do? What's the plan to break through the barriers once and for all?

13. **Simplify.** If a 10-year-old child were describing your product or service in "show and tell" at school, what would stand out in his/her mind? What is your plan to simplify and systematize what you do so that it is easier to REMEMBER?

14. **Make a New Face.** If you were to put a totally new face on your product or service, what would it be? Make it easier to SEE, easier to REMEMBER.

15. **Get Out.** Where is your biggest rut? What's the plan to get out fast?

16. **Climb.** Which is your tallest mountain? When does the expedition begin?

17. **End Comfort.** Where is your safest harbor? How can you make this a reliable base of operations and not merely a comfort zone?

18. **Shine.** Which is your brightest star? How will you remove the clouds that currently block the view? Call J-Lo.

19. **Dare to Dream.** If you could do anything you wanted to do with your business, what would it be? Where and when will you start? You can do anything. You can do everything. You just don't have to do it all at once. All you have to do is start somewhere.

20. **Seize the Moment.** What have others overlooked in your professional niche, marketplace, industry, or geographic region? What is your plan to seize the moment? Don't wait.

21. **Start a Revolution.** What pieces of a puzzle do you possess that could form the pattern of a revolutionary breakthrough for you and your customers—the next iPod or Google? What leverage will you bring to bear on the opportunity? Which partners will extend that leverage?

Break Through

There is energy in these questions. Read them all. Ponder them all. Start with question number one and then move to the next question that really turns on your creativity. These questions will be breakthrough questions for you. When someone asks, "And, how do you propose to do that?" Answer with the true optimist's answer: *Yes!* Yes means you don't have the detailed plan yet, but you will do what it takes to set the mark higher for your business as you prepare to positively *astonish* your customers. Finally, ask yourself and ask your team this 21st Century breakthrough question: What is theoretically possible? What is theoretically possible for our business in terms of impact, visibility, excellence, and growth?

Most individuals and organizations do not answer this question BOLDly enough. When someone says, "That's impossible," here's my answer. The truth is: *Nothing is impossible with the right partners.* If you doubt this, send me an email at darby@customerchampion.com. Tell me what it is you think is impossible and I'll send you a list of potential partners to contact. By the way, they're in the Yellow Pages and on the Internet.

Leverage and You

As you set lofty goals for your enterprise, what you will need is leverage to lift your world where you want it to be. At this point, let me introduce you to my other new book, ***LEVERAGE: How to Create Your Own Tipping Points in Business and in Life***, published by Career Press of Franklin Lakes, New Jersey. This insightful book and the one you now hold in your hand will guide you where you intend to go.

If you're ready for the next chapter, it's all about you…

- *You, the self-employed professional.*

- *You, the important frontline representative, the initial point of contact with each organization… In the eyes of the customer, you are "the organization" at the moment of contact.*

- *You, the owner of a small business.*

- *You, the manager and team leader of a dynamic department inside a large company.*

- *You, as a leader within your school system, government agency, professional association, or any other organization.*

You, as a dedicated professional and the leader of any enterprise that intends to positively *astonish* its customers…that intends to move from a listing in the phone book or from the cover of your brochure to the very *tops of the minds* of those who are waiting to discover what you do that will make their lives better. Be different. Be BOLD.

Chapter 4
Astonishing You

Why you? You are the one reading this book. You are the one who is becoming energized to create transformation in your business. You are the one others will look to as the example. You will lead the way. As the leader, you must instill a vision in others that will make it easy for them to positively *astonish* your customers. You must get that vision into the minds, hearts, *and the eyes* of your associates. Your success at accomplishing this will translate into an *astonishing* "Wow!" experience for your customers. This is the key to creating the positive, profitable, long-lasting relationships that will make your business "built to last." You will know you are successful when your customers can *look into the eyes of your associates and see the shared vision for your enterprise.* One team leader remarked, "With us, *Customer Astonishment* isn't something we do; it's something we have become."

It's All in the Eyes

So, you may ask, "What's all this about 'the eyes'?" As we each pursue our goals, we often focus on trying to figure out what we must DO to be successful. The more important quest may be to identify who we must BE to attract the success we desire. When I was a manufacturer's sales representative, I remember my savvy sales manager's advice, "Never let the customer see dollar signs in your eyes." As a young sales rep, I wondered if they could. Then, I realized that near the end of the fiscal quarter when I had not yet met my sales quota, I had dollar signs racing through my mind. This mental preoccupation probably translated into little infrared beams flashing dollar signs inside my eyeballs that said to the customer, "I need a sale. I need a sale. I need a sale." The more these little infrared beams flashed, the pushier I got, the more resistance I created, and the less I liked selling. So, I asked myself what it was that customers really needed to see in my eyes instead. Perhaps they needed to see a more *genuine interest* in them. Could they see it in my eyes, if I were interested in them or not? Aha, I needed to BE *interested*.

Could customers see in my eyes that I was enthused about my own products? I remember one sales seminar long ago when the instructor explained what the last four letters in the word *enthusiasm* stand for. He explained that "i-a-s-m" means "I am sold myself." Aha, I needed to BE *sold* on what I was selling.

Could my customers see in my eyes that I was scared? To be quite honest, sometimes I was under the gun to perform and somewhat afraid to disappoint my sales manager or my family. I needed to BE *brave*.

So, to succeed at sales and to succeed with my customers, I needed to BE interested, sold on my products, and brave, which meant more enthused and more confident that I had the ability to succeed. As I worked on these qualities and commitments, I believe the infrared dollar signs in my eyes turned to powerful energy beams that signaled my all-around confidence in what I was doing. Then, I could relax into selling and learn to enjoy *astonishing* my customers. Do you think they could see all this in my eyes?

How to Be

To DO stuff seems easier to pin down. To BE something is more intangible. Here's the important distinction: Instead of focusing right away on your handy to-DO list, discover the power of identifying what you need to BE. Then, you will recognize what you *truly must do* to make a lasting difference and a more genuine contribution to those you intend to *astonish*. Let me illustrate by using my own example as the young sales rep. The questions become...

A) What do individuals *do* to *be* genuinely *interested* in others?

B) What do individuals *do* to *be* truly *sold* on their own products?

C) What do individuals *do* to *be* clearly *brave* when selling?

Be Interested.

Here are the answers. In the customer care business, people who are INTERESTED in others study them in advance, learn about them, and take good notes when listening to them. They become world-class interviewers so that they can get beyond the symptoms of the customer's problems to the root causes—to connect *stated wants* with the *underlying needs* customers have.

I have always believed that a "leader is a reader of people." My dad was a salesman. I remember a fine speech he gave. Afterwards, a friend of his complimented him and said, "Widtsoe, you are obviously very well read." I was puzzled because I knew my dad actually didn't read that many books. There were a few good books he did read over and over again. So, I asked my dad, "Are you well read, Dad?" He replied, "Yes, son. Over my years in the selling profession, I have had the privilege of reading thousands of interesting people." I thought to myself, "How do you read people?" As the years have gone by, I have come to realize the fascinating truth of what he said. *Customer Astonishment is about reading people.*

Be Sold.

To be SOLD on your own products, you must study your products. You must use your own products. If you are not enthused about your products, you must work to improve them or find new ones. Perhaps you will become more SOLD on your products as you learn how very useful they are in ways you did not, at first, realize. To be truly SOLD on your products, you must move from merely selling the features and functions of your products to selling the BENEFITS of those products. This makes selling them more fun. And now you can connect being INTERESTED with being SOLD because you adapt the benefits of your products and services to what you truly understand your customers need, based on what you learned when you studied, interviewed, and really got to know them.

Be Brave.

To be BRAVE, you must believe in yourself first of all. What do you do to strengthen your belief in yourself and to be brave? You prepare. You pay attention in the sales seminar. You listen to your sales manager. You recognize that customers who challenge you or have objections are not rejecting you *personally*. You change your perception of these objections to see them as opportunities to further enlighten your customers or to learn from these so the next sale will be easier.

One powerful consultant who is a master at selling his services gave me this great analogy. If you are passionate (passionately interested in your customers or in love with your own great products), *you are on fire*. When the customer throws you an objection, it is as if they threw a log on the fire. You don't shrink from objections. You do not merely overcome objections. You *consume* objections as a fire would consume a log. The objection makes you more passionate about the value of the products and services you sell and more passionate about finding a way to encourage the customer who's not quite there yet.

Be More Powerful.

As you become interested in your customers, sold on your own products/services, and more brave, you will BE MORE POWERFUL. You will have the ability to make things happen. You will take the *10 Secrets to World-Class Customer Care* that follow and consume these to make your fire burn brighter and stronger.

Be the Brand.

Finally, you need to BE the brand. J-Lo is a brand. HP is a brand. Tiger Woods is a brand. iPod is a brand. You are a brand. And guess what, you are *already* distinct, different, and unique. Therefore, with the "You" brand, you have a head start. Build on what is distinctive, different, and unique about you. What is it? Please take a short break right now. Grab a notepad and a pen or turn on your word processor. Make a list of your unique experience, talents, perspectives, values, passions, skills, insights, and commitments—right here and now.

Be Your Best Self...Be the Example.

These unique qualities and capabilities you possess will further guide you to DO the right thing to assure success. This is to *BE the best version of who you are.* As a leader, you will enjoy this subtle twist… Here are the three most important things about BEING a great leader: Example, *example*, EXAMPLE. You must set the tone and set the pace for *Customer Astonishment*. This means that you will start by positively astonishing the members of your own work team—your INTERNAL customers.

Be Astonishing!

As you set out to *Be the Brand*, consider this career-building wisdom: "To succeed, figure out what you're really good at and do a lot of it." While it is great to expand your capabilities, don't under value the mastery you have already achieved in key areas. Stand for what you do well. Refine it. Then, expand on it. Be passionate about it. Create your own "value proposition" to support it. Connect it to what your customers truly need. Enjoy serving and *astonishing* them. Give of yourself. Make your everyday delivery of "you" extraordinary. Expect wonderful success. *And, realize that the greatest benefit your customers will derive from doing business with you is your commitment to them.*

You are *astonishing*!

Chapter 5
The Strategy

Some folks ask me if *Customer Astonishment* is just another buzz phrase or merely a philosophical label for a new way of thinking about customers. First of all, buzz phrases are not all bad, if they cause you to pay attention and to remember a concept. One of our company's largest training contracts came about simply because of the two words *Customer Astonishment*. I was teaching a public seminar at the Sheraton Hotel in Mesa, Arizona. A vice president of a major telecommunications company, who was not a seminar participant, happened to walk by the open door to our conference room and saw a slide with the two words up on the screen. He immediately called his assistant in New Jersey and said, "Please find out who's teaching a seminar at the Sheraton in Mesa on something called *Customer Astonishment* and get his contact information." He later told me he had been searching for new words to replace *customer service*. He and his associates were getting tired of the annual pitch *to improve customer service...to enhance customer service...to improve customer service.* He said his organization needed to stop improving *customer service* and replace the two words with a concept that would help to reinvent their approach to customers, not just improve it. He loved the energy inside the two words: *Customer Astonishment.* Thousands of his people later received our training.

The Customer Astonishment Grid

If *Customer Astonishment* were to become a label for your new philosophy for dealing with customers, this alone could be useful. A philosophy is a general set of beliefs that help to guide your actions. But, *Customer Astonishment* is much more than a buzz phrase or a philosophical label. It is a four-dimensional strategy for moving beyond traditional Customer Service to reinvent your approach. It will guide you as you plan for change and track your progress through four levels of customer awareness and customer care. The strategy is represented by the *Customer Astonishment Grid* that appears below. We will now discuss the genesis of the grid and the four distinct opportunities it represents for you and your team.

Please study the grid for a few minutes. Notice the two dimensions that define the quadrants within the grid. The vertical dimension is *Know...Sense* contrasted with the horizontal dimension, which is *Seize the Moment...Grow the Future*. Recognize that progression from one quadrant to another is from the lower-left Quadrant 1 up to Quadrant 2, then diagonally down to the lower-right Quadrant 3 and then up to Quadrant 4. This is the typical progression, in an N-like fashion, as individuals gain more skill and organizations become more sophisticated in addressing their customers' needs. Ultimately you will be serving your customers to the *Nth degree*! Wow!

	Seize the Moment	Grow the Future
S **e** **n** **s** **e**	Q2 The Opportunity to Build Loyalty — **ANTICIPATORY** — *Think AHEAD* *for the Customer*	Q4 The Opportunity to Lead the Way — **INTUITIVE** — *Think BEYOND* *the Competition*
K **n** **o** **w**	Q1 The Opportunity to Serve Well — **RESPONSIVE** — *Think ABOUT* *the Customer*	Q3 The Opportunity to Grow the Business — **EXPANSIVE** — *Think BIG* *about the Business*

As you continue to examine the grid, you will notice that each quadrant represents a distinct *opportunity* to impact your relationships with customers. Each quadrant has a *key word* in the center in bold capital letters. This is a *behavioral* word that suggests what you need to BE and DO to positively *astonish* your customers. These four words begin with the letters **R-A-E-I**, which will be symbolic as you learn more about the grid and this powerful multi-dimensional strategy. Finally, each quadrant represents a distinctive way of *thinking* about customer needs and the business opportunities you share with them.

Genesis of the Four Quadrants

The genesis of the grid is this. There are needs and wants that your customers articulate or *tell you* they need. Thus, you KNOW what they need. There are other things customers may need, which they do not articulate. Perhaps they forget to do so. Perhaps they didn't realize they needed something else. Perhaps it is a need they didn't know you could address. Thus, you can only observe the customer and hopefully SENSE that more is needed, based on what you see and on your previous experience in similar situations. As you think ABOUT your customers and also realize that, in a given situation, it is useful to think just AHEAD for them, you will *seize the moment* to assure success in the here and now. To illustrate: In a restaurant, the ordinary server who thinks ABOUT his customers provides bread and water at the beginning of the meal and then may wait until the customer requests more. A world-class server watches the bread basket and the water glasses and thinks AHEAD to replenish these before the customer has to ask. Which server will receive the larger tip?

The more you work with your customers, the more you will realize that there are other ways you can be of service to them that will help to *grow future business* with them. As you think BIG about the business, you will recognize parallel and related opportunities to support their needs. This is sometimes called cross-selling or recognizing that you can do more for the customer than may have initially been requested. The words "What else may I do for you today?" are very symbolic of this thinking BIG. This is often the key to *expanding* your business opportunity while providing an even more complete service to the customer. To illustrate: Consider the truck dealer that also sells trailer hitches and perhaps the trailers as well.

Ultimately, your best *intuition* will kick in as you help the customer see a bigger picture that allows them to *connect the dots* for their own success. Such thinking goes BEYOND the ordinary and beyond what your competitors offer. Your customers begin to look to you for more than service; they look to you for *leadership*. For example, back to the truck dealer. As you deliver the customer's shiny new truck with a trailer hitch, you also provide a friendly brochure with "Tips for Safe and Trouble-Free Towing." With such a complete strategy for addressing ALL of your customers' needs, your business will grow and thrive far into the future.

Let's now discuss each quadrant (Q1, Q2, Q3, and Q4) in more detail. Please take another careful look at the grid. I will now provide further illustrations and examples so that you can begin to operate multi-dimensionally in *astonishing* your customers. You are beginning to recognize that there is more to *Customer Astonishment* than a simple buzz phrase. There is the opportunity to master the "10 Secrets to World-Class Customer Care" that are based on this fundamental **R-A-E-I** strategy.

Quadrant 1: Be Responsive...Serve Well.

What is the opportunity that arises when the customer tells you what she needs—gives you an order, writes up a specification, etc.? It is the basic opportunity to do business, to fundamentally *serve the customer well*. At this point, your performance is not totally remarkable because it is about filling the basic requirements of doing business. It is doing what the customer expects you to do. However, Quadrant 1 is the foundation quadrant. If you can't take care of the basics, you certainly are not ready to move ahead to the other quadrants.

The way you lay the foundation for *Customer Astonishment* in this quadrant is to perform at a level of excellence and consistency that is exceptional. For example, you will not *astonish* your restaurant customers by cooking great steaks. They will be pleased, but not *astonished*. They expect great steaks, cooked with skill. What becomes especially important in order to create a powerful and lasting impression is that the steaks are equally tender and juicy night after night, week after week. And, when your customers send their friends to the restaurant, the result will be absolutely predictable. They'll find the same great steaks. Everybody will rave about the steaks. So, being *Responsive* is doing what you do very well to establish your overall credibility and then to do it with exceptional consistency so that the customer feels secure in relying on your products and services. You've laid the foundation for *Customer Astonishment*.

Quadrant 2: Be Anticipatory...Build Loyalty.

Here is where you really start to build momentum for *Customer Astonishment*. Beyond what the customer tells you she needs are those elements of service and support that the customer may forget to tell you or does not put into words. Quadrant 2 is your opportunity to *observe* your customers, to pay special attention to your customers, to anticipate their needs and act without waiting to be asked, whenever you sense a true need is there. I remember in 1991 when Japanese luxury sports sedans were coming onto the market in a big way: Lexus, Infiniti, and Acura. Each company was working hard to incorporate those extra features that would delight and *astonish* their customers and justify the incremental price of these vehicles. Even though I wanted to drive one of these cars, I decided they were too pricey for my budget at that point in time. I deferred my lease of an Infiniti until 1995. What I did in 1991 was to make a compromise. I chose to lease a Mitsubishi Diamante, which was quite sporty, but about $10,000 less than the other brands.

To this day, I remember the *Customer Astonishment* squeal of excitement from my young son as we zoomed along in my new Diamante one afternoon. The sun was shining from the west directly into the windshield. My son pulled down his visor. I pulled down mine. However, the sun was still beaming directly into my eyes over the top of the rearview mirror. I chuckled as I realized there was a little surprise feature to this new car that had never been in any previous car I had owned—a feature that most drivers on this sunny afternoon would wish they had. There was a tiny little visor just above the rearview mirror. I proudly pulled it down. My son was *astonished*. "Hey, that's way cool, dad. I've never seen that before. Who thought of that? That's awesome." These were the words of *Customer Astonishment*.

These tiny visors are more prevalent now, but, at the time, Mitsubishi had read my mind and had anticipated that moment when I would benefit from something I hadn't expected to find in my automobile. They had paid attention over the years and thought AHEAD for me to add a special little convenience that *smoothed the way* for me. Capture that phrase "smooth the way." Being anticipatory often has that primary impact for the customer. You smooth the way. This may be the restaurant server who doesn't wait to fill your water glass or bread basket. It is the computer manufacturer who includes the idiot-proof, quick-installation guide inside the top of the computer shipping carton. Being anticipatory is also VERY IMPORTANTLY about giving the customer OPTIONS. Stay tuned for Secret #10. In the final analysis, it is the collection of all the thoughtful, anticipatory, didn't-have-to-be-told things you do for customers that goes beyond servicing their needs *to servicing their loyalty*.

Quadrant 3: Be Expansive...Grow the Business.

Quadrant 3 challenges you to "think out of the box," as they say. With the *Customer Astonishment Grid*, you move to a new box (quadrant) in the new world of the Future. You increasingly realize that, in order to grow and expand business opportunities with your customers, you must move beyond your business comfort zone and not be stuck selling or serving only what you have always sold or served in the same old ways you have always sold or served it. This quadrant demands that you become an expediter. This is the world of providing your basic product along with offering accessories and supporting services of various kinds. At this point, the question often comes up, "What if we don't have accessories or the expertise to provide supporting services?" Sometimes the customer may ask for something that is "far out of the box" or far out of your comfort zone. The understandable temptation is to say to the customer, "I'm sorry, we don't offer that or we just can't do that." You may then look at your associates and say, "That's impossible." Well, here's a breakthrough of breakthroughs. *NOTHING is impossible in business (or life) with the right partners.*

Let me illustrate with a truly amazing story. I have a friend who lives in a developing nation with limited local resources. He is very entrepreneurial and has a reputation for being especially resourceful. His primary business is home electronics and entertainment systems. He has a friend who handles procurement for his country's small navy. This fellow approached him with the unusual need to acquire a large number of life jackets. Instead of saying, "I don't manufacture or sell life jackets," my friend asked for a day or two to investigate the availability of life jackets. He then went to his office where he had a stack of yellow-page telephone directories (not even an Internet connection) for most of the 50 United States of America. He knew that Minnesota had many lakes so he figured there would be many boats and the need for many life jackets. He telephoned several companies to get quotes on life jackets. He chose a supplier.

Several weeks later, my friend chartered a cargo jet to fly to Minneapolis to pick up the life jackets and returned home to fulfill the needs of his nation's navy. He got such a good deal on the life jackets that the cost of the jet was easy to include in his fair price to the Navy. His personal effort expended was merely a few phone calls and a round trip flight to Minneapolis. He made a tidy profit and established an entirely new business for himself. I have always been amazed by this story to realize how easy it is to find excuses for not going the extra mile for our customers. We tend to think on the small and the safe side of things and not think BIG enough. To be *expansive* is to see the BIG picture, to be resourceful, to subcontract, to adapt, to accessorize, and to find partners, partners, and more partners.

Here's my own personal account. I receive inquiries from individuals "out of the blue" who locate our company in the phone directory or on the Internet. They call about a very interesting range of training programs from "pet obedience" to "commercial driving" to "geriatric care" to "how to use Microsoft products." None of these course topics are among our own product offerings. However, I never say, "No, we don't offer that course." Instead I do three things…

1. Get more background on the need being expressed: Who is the training for? What is the learning objective? What is the preferred delivery format, etc.?

2. Ask for 30 minutes or perhaps 24 hours to check with our "various resources" and partners.

3. Then, do the research to find a potential partner, to locate an outside source from whom I can purchase training materials (books, videos, etc.) or to whom I can refer the inquirer, or to determine that we can create or contract with someone else to create a credible instructional program on "pet obedience."

The result is that the person who contacted me is amazed at my helpful attitude and general resourcefulness. Even if I refer them to someone else, they know who made the connection for them. And, often they come back to me for other training needs that are part of our core business. I do not paint myself into a box that says, "This is all we do." The day-to-day manifestation of problems with Quadrant 3 are these comments we all dread to hear, "Sorry, that's not my job" or worse yet, "Sorry, I just work here." I mentioned earlier that one of the scariest GHOSTs each company must eliminate is the perception by many of those on the front lines that they are not "business people."

The answer we want and need to hear is, "Let me check to see who can help you with that" or "Let me write down your request, name, and phone number so that someone can get back with you and find a way to help." This is staying open. This is being expansive.

Quadrant 4: Be Intuitive…Lead the Way.

When you and your associates get to this fourth dimension of the R-A-E-I grid, you will have achieved what we talked about in Chapter 3. You will have earned a place at the *tops of the minds* of your customers. They will have benefited from your service excellence and more. They will know you are paying attention to their needs and bringing many resources to bear on solving their problems, satisfying their needs, and exceeding their expectations.

When you reach Quadrant 4, you are the professional, the company, the college, the government agency to watch, to benchmark, to listen to. You will be seen as leading the way. And, rather than wait until they need a product or service, these customers will consult you for recommendations as they plan their own business strategies and design their own products and services. For example, if you were going to sell products on line via the Internet, which companies would you like to consult first? Would the list include Amazon.com and eBay? If you were going to launch a "personal management" software product, would you benchmark Intuit Corporation? If you planned to open a chain of restaurants, would you like to talk to the folks who run the Outback Steakhouses?

What makes all of these companies you wish to consult special is that, in order to pioneer their product/service niche, they each had to see PATTERNS that others did not see. And, due to their excellent track records in running their businesses in competitive environments, they have determined the PATTERNS of success that others hope to emulate. Being *Intuitive* is about seeing patterns that others miss. It is about *connecting the dots*, so to speak, that lets you leapfrog the competition with a complete product or service strategy long before others have "broken the code."

If you are one of these companies, you are seen as breaking through the obstacles and breaking through the ordinary to give your customers something special that gives them a real advantage, in turn. Here, are two examples of being *Intuitive* you will recall. Once upon a time, Sony made boom boxes for bookshelves. Their engineers traveled to America to see these in use and observed teenagers carrying these on their shoulders as they shimmied and shuffled along the sidewalks. Instead of providing a shoulder pad and a Velcro strap to tie the device to the user's head so he wouldn't drop it, a miniature boom box was born called the Walkman. Sony had recognized an important pattern other manufacturers had missed.

You know the rest of the story. Along came iPod. But, Steve Jobs tells another story about "intuitive insight"—an important pattern Apple almost *missed*. With the advent of iTunes, Apple engineers were on top of the world. Teenagers and the rest of us were downloading music from the Internet, paying Apple for its use, and avoiding the less personalized and inconvenient process of making a trip to the music or bookstore. Apple iTunes customers were downloading and burning their own CDs, then putting these in their Discman CD players. Cool. Steve Jobs says they almost missed it. What? Answer: the nuisance of burning a CD. Why not download the music directly into a miniature player with its own memory chip? And, the iPod was born.

On an everyday note, consider this great example: When visiting Douglas, Arizona, on business with my wife, Sharon, we joined our client and her spouse for dinner. We chose to dine at the Mexican restaurant located in the Gadsden Hotel in the downtown district of this colorful and historic community. Our server was a young man about 20 years of age. He introduced himself and proceeded to take our orders. We asked a few questions about the menu. He explained that the House Specialties included a dinner roll and a salad. He noted that the sandwich plates and the traditional Mexican dishes included garnishes, but no salad. However, a salad was just $1.95 additional.

Three of us quickly ordered from the House Specialties side of the menu. As we did, our server asked us for our choices of salad dressings. Sharon was the last to order and chose the Mexican Combo plate #8. Our server paused for just a second and then said, "Ma'am, your friends will all be having salads before the main course. I would like to also bring you a salad with my compliments, if you wish." WOW! We were all *astonished* at this young man's thoughtfulness and foresight. Sharon thanked him for his generosity. Such a simple gesture, and yet, this extra salad demonstrated not only our server's concern for his guests but his realization that the goodwill he would create would ultimately be far more valuable than the proceeds from the sale of $1.95 salad.

We assumed that the young man had acted with the blessing of his restaurant manager. Our perception was that his behavior was a reflection of the true spirit of the establishment. Had he merely mentioned the salad to Sharon and asked her if she would like to add one for $1.95, he would have been thinking ahead. By offering the salad with his compliments, he was thinking BIG about the business. But, what was most important was his fundamental intuition about my wife's situation that allowed him to see more. He was concerned that she would be sitting there watching her three companions eat their crispy, colorful salads and perhaps feel left out. At that point, he had leapfrogged the average restaurant and the average server. What was the result of this multi-dimensional act of *Customer Astonishment*? The story found its way into this fantastic new book on world-class customer care. And, if you're ever in Douglas, Arizona, where are you going to go for dinner? Answer: the Mexican restaurant at the historic Gadsden Hotel.

In Conclusion

The first four chapters set the stage and prepared you for the 10 Secrets. This chapter is the pivotal chapter in causing you to identify a more strategic and complete approach to the needs and wants of your customers. Make a mental connection with **R-A-E-I**. Ask yourself as you examine your own customer care procedures and practices, am I / are we *Responsive, Anticipatory, Expansive*, and *Intuitive* in addressing the needs of our customers? When you have your next customer-focused team conversation, realize that you will automatically think ABOUT your customers. Remind yourselves to also think AHEAD, think BIG, and think BEYOND for your customers. The results will be beneficial to ALL who are involved, including you.

In conclusion, here are four simple checklists to guide you in your **R-A-E-I** commitments. The 10 Secrets will dovetail with and support these checklists.

To Be More Responsive...

- Design your place of business to be a very pleasant and comfortable place to do business.

- Send especially clear signals of appreciation to all customers and especially to your "priority customers."

- Eliminate any DLTWIDs (Re-read Chapter 2).

- Learn more about your customers—as individuals, as organizations, or as a so-called market segment.

- Solicit customer feedback formally and informally on a regular basis.

- Do regular benchmarks of other organizations in the same business as yours.

- Pay attention to the details.

To Be More Anticipatory...

- LISTEN carefully. Pay attention to the customer. Be aware of both verbal and non-verbal communication.

- Provide the customer with options.

- Smooth the way wherever you can, from simpler forms to fill out, to doors that open easily, and far more.

- Make sure no customer is left out, overlooked, or somehow loses out in the process of doing business with you.

- Address any *Systemic* or *Cultural* factors that may get in the way of *Customer Astonishment*. These could be a telephone system that malfunctions (Systemic) or a rush, rush atmosphere in the office where folks forget to say "please" and "thank you" (Cultural).

- When you get to Secret #10, study the A-C-T technique thoroughly. It is at the heart of being a world-class problem solver in *astonishing* your customers. Let it become a habit to A-C-T.

- Seize those *Moments of Truth* when you do not get a second chance to make a first impression. See Secret #7.

To Be More Expansive...

- Ask the customer: "Is there anything else we can do for you today?"

- Examine the completeness of your product or service offering? Where can you enhance it? What accessories or supporting services can you also make available to the customer? Be "one-stop shopping," wherever you can. Integrate your services with those of other professionals or organizations.

- Network. Locate important resources. Find more partners who will be on-call to assist you with unusual and exciting customer needs that arise to stretch your imagination and expand your capabilities.

- Generally, be a world-class expediter: "If we don't have the solution, we'll find it for you and connect you to the right resource to get the job done."

- Safeguard your *Chain of Customers*. See Secret #2.

- Ask the 21st Century question: "What is theoretically possible in terms of the quality, affordability, timeliness, friendliness, completeness, etc...of our products and services?"

To Be More Intuitive...

- Keep your customers informed. Tell them what you know that will contribute to their success. Don't wait for them to call or email you.

- Interpret your Core Purpose, as a business, very broadly. For instance, if you run a dance studio, it's not just about teaching dance steps. It's about the joy of movement and music and romance and self-confidence and having a good time. Besides dance lessons, you can sell audio CDs and refreshments. You may choose to partner with a Yoga institute or a dating service.

- Scan for patterns. Don't discount the unusual things you see. Make note of these. These are the pieces of a larger puzzle that you will one day assemble to become your new competitive advantage.

- Turn on the learning. Read. Attend seminars and conferences. Take a night class at the local community college.

- Experiment. Be brave. Try new things. To fail once or twice is to learn. To fail repeatedly at the same thing is not smart. As Tom Peters says, "Re-Imagine!"

- Get away from familiar surroundings from time to time to just THINK.

- Reinvent your capabilities, individually, and as an organization.

- Learn to expect the unexpected and don't be afraid. Be prepared.

- Do your dreams. Your customers will be inspired and want to do business with you.

R-A-E-I: *Customer Astonishment* is much more than a buzz phrase. Get ready for the "10 Secrets." Secrets to what, you may ask? These are the secrets to building on your "culture of service excellence" to become the most professional and powerful version of who you are. Why are these secrets? The answer: Because not everybody will seize the opportunity to put them to work. As *you* do, others will realize that you have discovered something that makes your products and services extraordinary.

Section II: 10 Secrets

Secret #1

Be Customer Champions!

Everybody loves a champion. We know champions as skillful experts and courageous heroes. They inspire us. We are sorely disappointed when one of them lets us down by a behavior that is out of character with their greatness and achievement. We expect our champions to stand for something...physical prowess, endurance, a keen eye, a quick mind, determination, creativity, perseverance, and certainly excellence. When I think of physical prowess and endurance, I immediately recall the televised stories of Bruce Jenner's preparation to win the Decathlon event at the 1976 Olympic Games. I was much younger and more impressionable at the time. It was amazing to me that someone would so totally dedicate himself to being the best. I remember that he ran, jumped, hurdled, vaulted, heaved, and tossed for eight or more hours every day for months on end. When I think of a keen eye and creativity, John Nieto comes to mind. As I visit the art galleries in the magical city of Sedona, Arizona, I stand in awe at the energy that radiates from his unique paintings. These individuals are heroes to me. Each stands for something special. Such individuals set a mark for us all to admire, perhaps envy, and possibly to strive for.

No, I'm Increasing My Tips.

What is your standard of excellence? What do you stand for? When do you demonstrate strength and endurance? When is your keen eye and creativity evident? I remember sitting outside a restaurant at the Philadelphia airport just before it opened for dinner at 5:00. Through the glass, I could see the headwaiter with a cloth in one hand and a bottle of cleaning solution in the other. He was going from table to table polishing the dinnerware and checking the rim of each glass on every table. When the restaurant opened, I walked right up to the gentleman and said, "I bet I know what you're doing— you're taking pride in your work." He turned quickly and said, "No, I'm increasing my tips." Either way, he knew that his keen eye for hard water spots on a spoon or a lipstick smudge on the rim of a glass could make or break the dining experience for some customer he was about to serve. Whatever his motivation, he had high standards when it came to the appearance of his table settings. He stood for something that translated into a better dining experience for his customers and a more lucrative evening for himself and his associates. Most importantly, his customers would return.

For what championship qualities will you be known? What will determine your reputation in the eyes of your customers?

What Goes Around Comes Around.

We are disappointed when someone lowers the standard. Then, the word travels and "championship" is called into question. I recently had a friend recommend a place of business and then say something like this, "If a woman named Marge answers the phone, hang up or ask to be transferred to anybody else. The company's great, but she's a real pain to deal with." When we disappoint our customers, we have failed to champion their needs and to put them on the pedestal they generally deserve. A *customer champion* is one who looks out for his or her customers…someone who works to a higher standard to please their customers and who becomes a champion in their eyes. What goes around comes around. In business and in life, *we teach people how to treat us*.

Is the Rhythm Steady…Is the Pulse Strong?

The heart of a champion is strong. It beats with a steady rhythm. It creates a strong pulse. What is at the heart of your commitment to customers? Is the rhythm steady? Is the pulse strong? Those who serve others well do so on the basis of some *Core Purpose* they sense and that others may miss. One of my clients is an Information Systems support group inside a major municipality. They have a technician who is known as the "stealth technician." Why? He always works on his customers' computers when they are away from their offices so he doesn't have to deal with them face to face. Then, when they return to find their computer has been fixed, they call to learn what the problem was and what this fellow did to correct it. The stealth technician never returns their phone calls. So, as competent as he is, he generates a disproportionate share of the customer complaints. When confronted about not returning customer phone calls, he says, "Why should they complain, their computer works doesn't it?" The customers feel left in the dark. The subtle importance of customer communication is totally overlooked by this fellow whose *customer care pulse* is weak.

We recognize those among us who are champions and those who are not. If Bruce Jenner chose to omit practicing the long jump, we would ultimately be shocked when his Decathlon performance fell short. If John Nieto left a smudge on the corner of a painting priced at $5,000 or $50,000, we would be appalled. Similarly we are disappointed when the technician doesn't return our phone calls or when a waiter leaves a lipstick smudge on the rim of a glass. We expect customer champions.

It may be too easy to rationalize that Bruce Jenner and John Nieto are highly paid and should be expected to "take more pride in their work" than a computer technician or restaurant server might be expected to do. This rationalization fails as we recognize that Bruce Jenner's wealth came after he proved himself a champion. John Nieto had to paint well enough to sell any paintings at all—for perhaps $75 or $200—before his work would be displayed in the prestigious galleries of Sedona. Bruce and John's spirit of championship had to be cultivated and allowed to develop in order to gradually build their reputations for excellence. Then, the rewards came.

So, what is the secret? If it's aerobic exercise that builds your heart muscle, what do you do to pump up your Core Purpose and the spirit of championship? Where does it begin? How will you help your team strengthen their commitment to a winning performance and to service excellence? How will you achieve your own Olympic best and gain the recognition you desire? Here are some proven ideas to guide you.

Business Is Better with Bookends.

Occasionally, I decide to put a few extra books on the very top of a piece of furniture, without the benefit of regular bookshelf walls to the left and to the right. Of course, the books tend to fall over eventually and often end up hitting me on the head to remind me of the folly of *living life without bookends.*

I use this analogy with my clients: You wrote the book(s) on your business. You have your business plan, your sales manual, your HR policies, your blueprints, and other "books" that reflect your various areas of expertise and functional responsibility. If these books of yours stand all alone on the top of the bookshelf, they will collect dust and they will most likely fall down or out of alignment without bookends.

Your organization and your team must have bookends. From my experience, the most useful bookends are these: On the left of the books, you will have a strong sense of your *Core Purpose* and on the right of your books you will have a very clear *Customer Focus.* With your purpose in mind and a clear commitment to your customers, you will be guided to "do the right thing" and you will find that the books on your bookshelf stay in alignment." Here is the illustration…

Let's discuss Core Purpose, how you define it, crystallize it, and use it to build the spirit of customer championship. Begin by considering this question: Somewhere at the center of what's going on inside your business, there is a reason for it all—a driving force that keeps you going from day to day and year to year…What is it? It makes little sense to direct your focus to caring for customers if you are not sure WHY the fundamental work you do is important—to them and to you. When and where and how are your customers counting on you? These questions are also clues to the ultimate question: Why is your work important to others?

I once visited a company that manufactures brass fittings for hydraulic hoses. There was much emphasis on process control and product quality. WHY? If you were a brass fittings assembler, you may figure the purpose was to just make good fittings so you could sell a bunch of these and make some profit. Or, if you happened to know that one of the principal applications of these fittings was on the hydraulic hoses that helped to operate aircraft landing gear, your perception of purpose might be deepened. Suddenly your purpose might become *to build failure-proof fittings to keep air travelers safe and to lead the way with quality products in your industry*. With this commitment and effective management of your operations overall, you would meet your profit goals.

Key Words to Signify What You Stand For

Involve your team in a discussion of the underlying importance of what you do. Derive a statement of purpose that will empower your day-to-day work activities. Once an organization's Core Purpose is in motion, it becomes the impetus for building the reputations that distinguish great organizations. Here are some examples to tease your thinking. Quick Note: Try not to peek ahead as I ask you this question: Which companies come to mind when I say these key phrases: (a) **family fun**, (b) **affordable air travel**, and (c) **safe cars**?

- **Disney** has built their reputation on making sure families have fun.

- **Southwest Airlines** makes air travel safe, dependable, *and* consistently affordable.

- **Volvo** has focused its reputation on protecting your family with safe vehicles.

The dedication to purpose of these companies is evident to most of us. For all the efforts of other car manufacturers to get good safety ratings, Volvo practically owns the word "safe." Southwest owns "affordable." Disney may not own "fun" all by itself, but they could be said to own the words, "family fun." These are the reasons these companies exist. The more the people inside each organization understand the Core Purpose, feel it, and live up to it, the more successful the organization becomes. For what will your team be so known? What are the Key Words you may own one day?

Take a stroll around your office at the next break. Ask several employees what they believe to be the central purpose for what they do—for what your organization does. Make note of the answers. Some will surprise you. Some will delight you. The combination of these will come together to allow you to create a draft for further discussion and eventual ratification by your team. Some people may shrug their shoulders and say, "I haven't a clue." Please reserve judgment. They may be hard workers who have not yet contemplated the idea of "purpose." Others may not care. Some of your associates will be grateful that you are taking the time to clarify the importance of their work. You must decide what the value of a clearer sense of purpose will be so that you can stay the course and build a more purposeful organization. The result will be greater loyalty all around.

Building Commitment to Your Core Purpose

This is going to take some work—satisfying work. The law of averages says that some of your associates are "just doing their jobs." This is important, but it isn't enough if *Customer Astonishment* is your goal. Why is this not enough? It has been said that a machine or computer can do the work of 50 ordinary men and women, but NO MACHINE can do the work of a single *extraordinary* man or woman. So, the answer to the question "why is this not enough" is another question: Do you intend to be ordinary or extraordinary? I do not believe you would be reading this book if the answer were not *extraordinary*. Here are some further tips for making your Core Purpose an idea of real substance and impact, and part of your "corporate DNA"…

Tip #1: Folklore. A number of years ago, I spent a day in Wichita, Kansas, with the great Coleman Company. I was impressed to learn that the company actually employed a historian. He was the curator of the company museum. There is much powerful folklore surrounding the Coleman family of products dating back to World War I, including the tiny, absolutely reliable, portable stove that every soldier considered to be among his prize possessions. What is your team's folklore? Are there legendary customer rescue missions to recount? Who among your seemingly ordinary colleagues may be idolized by a customer who swears by the product (or process) your teammate designed? Get the folklore going. Have a quarterly get-together to celebrate your recent triumphs and current successes.

Tip #2: Customer Panel. Create a Customer Panel with rotating membership. Invite these customers to attend a semiannual meeting with your employees to tell them what they like about you, your services and products—how you have helped them. Take a smaller percentage of time to let them explain how you could support them more fully. This is not to be a complaint session. The customers will understand. Properly selected and invited, the customers will be eager to fuel your team's excitement.

Tip #3: Decision Making. Signal to the world that your Core Purpose, along with your organization's mission statement, are prime criteria for key decisions. When it comes time to rearrange the office layout, ask, "Will this arrangement make it easier to fulfill our Core Purpose?" When you design the next promotional piece to advertise your products, ask, "Does this promo piece also represent to our customers *what we stand for* as an organization?" When you prepare to hire a new team member, ask, "Does this person understand our Core Purpose? Will she/he contribute to it?"

Tip #4: Recognition and Rewards. A number of years ago, Michael LeBoeuf wrote a book entitled *GMP: Greatest Management Principle in the World*. The timeless principle is simply: *people do what gets rewarded*. This is not a mercenary concept. Yes, money is part of the equation, but the real core of the concept is that we are all creatures of positive reinforcement. While you have naturally occurring motives to do a good job, you certainly appreciate being appreciated. You are pleased when someone notices the effort you expended and the contribution you made. Take time as teammates to recognize each other and be sure that your reward systems take into account those worthy accomplishments that move your Core Purpose toward its fulfillment.

Consider the following anecdote as you examine the importance of your Core Purpose, as you set out to meet the needs and exceed the expectations of your customers.

The Vacation of a Lifetime

You are on a jungle safari. You are in search of your own *gorillas in the mist*. You will collect a diary full of stories to tell your grandchildren. You have hired an experienced guide named Charles who is a perfectly amicable fellow. He walks briskly, helps you over fallen logs, and even carries a state-of-the-art global positioning gadget. After two days in the jungle, you ask him, "Where are we going next?" He replies, "I'm not exactly sure, but I do know our current position." On the third day, Charles appears weary. You ask him why and he says, "This is my 17th safari this year. Thank goodness it's Friday, I can hardly wait till Saturday when we'll take a rest." Shocked, you ask, "Just what do you think is the purpose of this trip?" His answer, "I haven't thought that much about it, but our safari company needs the revenue and the owners would be really ticked off if we didn't get in four more safaris by the end of the year." How do you feel about now? All of Charles' experience, his friendliness, and his GPS gadgets are overshadowed by his lack of purpose. **You and he are disconnected.**

Purposeful Energy

The jungle safari story should illustrate the importance of knowing your purpose as you serve others. Such purpose is a source of energy. This energy comes from the knowledge that you are providing *something you believe in* to someone else who needs it and that you will both reap the rewards. Ask yourself what might be in conflict with your own sense of Core Purpose. What distracts you? Let's suppose you are engaged in one of those all-too-common business meetings where at first you may be bored and then you do become intrigued with all the "hidden agendas" that are beginning to emerge. Someone is promoting a new marketing strategy. Someone else reminds the group of budget constraints.

Then someone attempts to justify adding more people. What is the answer? Imagine that your most important customer suddenly walks into the room, smiles, and asks what is going on. Would the tone of the meeting change? Could the customer's mere presence remind you of certain priorities that would help to resolve your internal conflicts? It could be useful to ask yourselves next time you're stuck in such a team discussion: What would be our customers' perspective on all this? Consider this *Customer Astonishment* Motto...

If it supports our Core Purpose and the customer needs it, we do it! All else may be of secondary importance.

As we conclude this section and encourage you and your team to stay focused on the Core Purpose, please consider the following definition of "customer."

CUSTOMER: The individual or organization next in line to receive *value added* as a result of the performance of my/our work; the individual or organization that purchases the product of my/our labors or who funds our enterprise.

In this book, we will consider issues and opportunities that pertain to both your internal and your external customers. We will not differentiate between these as to which is more important than the other. If you do, you will find that you have a double standard for service, which will backfire. Why? Here is a key principle: *If you are not now serving the end customer, you are serving someone who is.* How you serve the person who is next in line affects their ability to serve who's next after them. Ultimately, there is a ripple effect that impacts the end customer. Or, as they might say in the military, whatever gets poured on your helmet may splash on the customer.

Get your team together and consider your Core Purpose. Let it be the bedrock foundation of your overall standards of excellence. Let it be as the heart of the excitement you feel for your work. Here are some criteria to help you define it...

1. Does the statement of Core Purpose look at your work from the customer's perspective?

2. Is it something that adds both importance and excitement to the work you do even though some tasks may be routine? (Remember the aircraft hydraulic hose fittings assembler who protects the lives of air travelers?)

3. Does the statement make you feel included?

4. Is it short, concise, and easy to remember?

5. Can you *buy in* to make it part of your commitment to the work you do?

6. Does it "stoke your fire" and "ring your chimes"?

7. Could it cause you to wake in the morning and spring to your feet?

As the author, here's my Core Purpose in serving (even *astonishing*) you:

...To embolden you to distinguish yourself from the crowd, to build powerful business relationships, to positively astonish your customers, to have more fun, and to make some serious money.

Business relationships do make the world go around. Customers give us the opportunity to apply our talents to serve them. Then, they let us transfer money from their bank accounts to ours so that we have the financial leverage to meet our goals. And, in summary, *as your work becomes more purposeful*, everything works together much more smoothly and more powerfully for all who are involved. You become the customer's champion. The whole thing becomes a really big WIN / WIN!

Secret #2
Get Connected!

In my business, travel is part of the plan. When our children were younger, I tried to alternate my long trips with weeks where I could be mostly home. On those occasional weeks when I would be gone through a Saturday morning, I would stop by the local 41-flavors doughnut shop on the way home from the airport to buy a special treat for my kids. One Saturday morning, I got in line behind a fellow who had never made a decision prior to that point in his life. He began by asking the sales clerk for a half-dozen doughnuts and as he noticed one new deep-fried sensation after another, he expanded his order to a full dozen, then to two dozen. He repeatedly modified his order in this fashion: "Ooh, those pink ones look yummy, add a couple of those. I see you've got some new twisty ones with caramel frosting. Throw in a couple of those. And, you'd better put back a couple of those glazed ones."

The Day of the Doughnut Sorter

The line of prospective customers behind me began to grow. The young clerk at the front counter was perishing though somehow managing to stay pleasant. I admit I was in a hurry to get home and was becoming exasperated with this fellow's elongated doughnut selection process. I looked around the shop for assistance. There was the cook with his hands covered in dough. He was indisposed. Then, I noticed in the back corner of the shop a "doughnut sorter." This young person was carefully arranging the pink ones on one shelf and the twisty frosted ones on another shelf of a stainless steel doughnut cart. I looked in the front counter to be sure it was full and then felt justified in clearing my throat somewhat loudly and giving a friendly wave to the doughnut sorter. He saw me, smiled a big grin, and waved back. Then, he continued sorting doughnuts.

I was astounded. I worked to restrain my natural instincts. In my mind, there should be no such thing as a "doughnut sorter." Cross training in doughnut sorting, yes. But, *everybody* in such a busy, customer-focused place of business needs to be a *doughnut server*. This one young man was obviously disconnected from what I call the **Chain of Customers**. Is doughnut sorting important? Of course it is. However, if the front counter is fully supplied and something has blocked the flow of doughnuts to eagerly waiting customers, unblocking that flow should very quickly become the number one priority of everybody in the shop.

From Chain of Command to Chain of Customers

This *Chain of Customers* is not only about connecting with your *external* customers; it is very much about the effectiveness of your work team and your relationships with other *internal* customers. A Chain of Customers can be contrasted with the traditional *Chain of Command*. A Chain of Command is very efficient in times of war and in times of emergency, but it is not always conducive to individual initiative and team creativity. Let me illustrate. Very often, a seminar participant or the employee of a client company will approach me with a question. The conversation often begins like this, "Mr. Checketts, I'm *just* a technician at Acme Corporation and I was wondering..." Or, "Darby, I'm *just* an administrative assistant here at the college and I've noticed..." About 50% of the employees out there introduce themselves to me with some variation of the words "just a." That's an interesting job title, a "justa." Where do they get this? In a hierarchical organization (chain of command), technicians and administrative assistants are at or near the bottom of the pyramid. The chain of command leads to the "big boss" and many employees feel like a "justa." With a Chain of Customers, there are certainly NO unimportant links. And, guess where the Chain of Customers leads? It leads to the "real boss." Who is everybody's real boss? Answer: the end customer—the individual or organization who purchases the product of your labors or who funds your enterprise. And, remember: *If you are not now serving the end customer, you are serving someone who is.*

Team Linkage Protector

To develop a more customer-focused mindset, I encourage individuals to rename what they do at work. This new name or title may not show up on the organizational chart or your business card right away, but it will have a place in your head and in your heart as you consider how you affect those who depend on you for service. Too often, traditional JOB titles are about "things and processes" and are not descriptive of what people actually contribute. For instance, I had one administrative assistant speak up and say, "I am not just an *admin*. I am the *Team Bureaucracy Buster*." Seven of her teammates were in the room and they cheered as she declared her true contribution. What about the title of "supervisor"? The next-in-line customers of any supervisor are his/her team members. The title of "supervisor" is a very traditional one and speaks of the Chain of Command. In the context of the Chain of Customers, a supervisor becomes the *Team Linkage Protector*. Her job is to be sure that each member of the team *is* and feels *connected* so that there is a shared responsibility for keeping the doughnuts flowing smoothly to those customers who are eagerly waiting.

The Inverted Pyramid

Let's consider the end customer's perspective on all of this. The customer doesn't really care much about the organizational hierarchy unless a problem needs to be escalated. When they meet a representative of your organization, it is as if the org chart (the pyramid) is inverted. The person at the point of contact is the most important person in your organization at that moment. The customer would assume that all those above him or connected in the chain behind him are there to support the interaction that will occur at that point of contact.

Your Chain of Customers

Take a minute to draw your own Chain of Customers on a notepad. Draw it horizontally on the page, from left to right. Do you know which individuals and/or organizations precede you in the chain and which follow immediately and farther down the chain? What do you need from those who precede you? How do you let them know? What is most important to those who follow you in the chain? What do they need and expect from you? What is the process whereby *they* communicate this to you? How do you stay in touch with them to know how well you're doing? What can you do to improve the communication with your internal and your external customers?

Customer Communication

Would you believe that in the thousands of interactions I have had with various teams over the years, if I ask what serious obstacles they must overcome, one of the answers is almost always "communication problems"? Does this sound familiar? Why is communication such a big deal? There are two very big reasons. One will not surprise you. The other reason is too easy to overlook. First of all, communication is important because *people need information to do their work*. The second reason has to do with RESPECT. Quite frankly, we communicate most reliably with those whom we respect. For example, imagine you're in a hurry on your way back from a key meeting. There are some people you make a point to see and to tell what you've just learned that may be important to them. There are people you overlook and forget to tell what happened in the meeting. They may feel left out. And, there may be a few who are relieved that you didn't burden them with more information. As you pass the desks of some and stop at the desks of others, you are signaling who is important to you in the current course of events. As you keep others informed or seek their input, you show your respect for them. Therefore, if communication doesn't happen, it is a problem—often a big problem. The Chain of Customers is broken.

One Thing

Let's begin this discussion on the *inside* of your organization where the pattern of communication is set that will ultimately determine how well you communicate with those *external* customers. We'll begin with your team. Several years ago, I was teaching a teamwork seminar in London. A gentleman came up during the break and said, "Darby, I got just one thing out of your seminar." (For a moment I was concerned until I realized how important ONE THING could be.) He continued, "I have realized that our organization needs to have more *conversations* and fewer meetings." What is the difference between a conversation and a meeting? A conversation is two-way, more "personal," less formal, and usually more open. Does your team need to have some key conversations? The result of truly honest and productive team conversations is that you can *agree in principle* on what your team "stands for," how you will handle the natural conflicts that arise, and what kind of reputation you will create with your customers by how you communicate with them. When you communicate, you help your team get to the truth about situations, relationships, and opportunities. A thought worth pondering is this: *Effective teams get to the truth. Great teams get to the truth faster.*

Customer Conversations

Speaking of conversations, the most meaningful feedback you will ever get from your customers is not by way of surveys and questionnaires. These are useful for very specific purposes, but the best "customer data" is whatever the customer chooses to tell you as *his/her story* of what it is like to do business with you, your team, and your organization. It is called "anecdotal data gathering." It means that you must create opportunities for the customer to just chat with you to candidly share personal insights and those "little experiences" that really add up to the reputation you have with your customers. Become a *world-class interviewer* and take notes as you engage your customers in these key conversations.

Friendly Tips to Guide Your Conversations

Tip #1: Support Your Team. After the gentleman in London approached me about conversations, I decided that I needed to create a mechanism to guide teams in having those important conversations that would build unity, increase productivity, and help them raise the bar for customer care. The result was a friendly, 40-page guidebook entitled *29 Questions That Will Energize Your Team*. The guidebook is a useful companion to this book and is available at our Web site: www.CustomerAstonishment.com or as an e-book at Amazon. The 29 Questions have been carefully researched over years of team building to guide your team in creating a "culture of service excellence." A succinct summary of the 29 Questions appears below.

1. Who are our internal & external customers?
2. What is truly important to us as a team?
3. What is our VISION, incl. our Core Purpose?
4. What is our MISSION?
5. What do we honestly believe about our mission?
6. How will we know when we've succeeded?
7. What type of team are we? (4 types)
8. What is the optimum organization of our team?
9. What is each team member's unique role?
10. On what key relationships will we depend?
11. On what critical resources will we depend?
12. What are our performance goals?
13. What are our plans...our budget, etc.?
14. What roadblocks will we encounter?
15. How will we eliminate the Pride Killers?
16. What growth, dedication, and skill will be required?
17. How will we assure continuous learning?
18. For what shall our team be known?
19. Where can we make "process improvements"?
20. How will we be recognized and rewarded?

21. How will we assure quality of work life and balance?
22. How will we value individuality and diversity?
23. How will we handle our conflicts?
24. How will we manage change?
25. What conversations will we need to have regularly?
26. How will we make the work enjoyable—even fun?
27. How will we handle stress—even failure?
28. How will we celebrate our successes?
29. What else needs to be discussed—any loose ends?

In working with hundreds of organizational teams, I have learned this interesting principle: **Great teams learn to talk about what they may *need to* talk about *before* they *have to* talk about it.** Please read that again slowly. It will catch on. Great teams get to the truth before it's too late. Ordinary teams hit the wall and wonder what happened. Great teams may hit the wall, but they quickly switch their approach to "Plan B," which they have previously talked about before they actually needed to use it. In the introduction to the *29 Questions* guidebook, there are instructions for prioritizing those questions that are most important and urgent for your team. The sooner you answer these, the stronger your Chain of Customers will be. *You will have talked about what you needed to talk about before you had to talk about it.*

Tip #2: Keep It Simple. You will also have opportunities for key conversations with your external customers. Be ready. Create a simple little "get the customer talking" feedback format to use on a daily basis as you interact with customers who are purchasing your products or perhaps meeting with you to review your service commitments. It can be as simple as four questions…

A. Did our performance and products meet your needs and expectations?

B. Were our products and/or services delivered in a timely manner?

C. Are our products/services a good value?

D. Where could we improve or expand our service to you in the future?

With questions A, B, and C, you are interested in the "yes" or "no" responses, but the main idea is to get the customer talking. Remember the anecdotal data gathering we talked about earlier. If you ask one of the questions and the customer begins to tell you a little story, be all ears. Take notes. Notice the customer's non-verbal language. If the customer is uncertain and hesitates in giving an answer, consider this to be a key learning opportunity. Politely say, "I noticed you hesitated slightly. Perhaps there is some special situation we need to resolve for you." And, if the customer has a complaint, tell her/him how much you truly appreciate the feedback!

Tip #3: Be Proactive. Don't wait to communicate. One of our clients is a small software company in Southern California. They practice what they call the *7-14-30 Rule*. After they install software for a client, they make an inviolable commitment to call that customer on the 7th day, the 14th day, and the 30th day after the installation. These are crucial points at which things will be settling in and going well or not. They do not simply wait until the customer calls as this often represents a "reactive" situation prompted by a problem that has arisen, which could have been prevented through regular dialogue with the customer.

I will often hear one of my client's say, "Our customers are always dropping bombshells on us, with a new request or sudden demand that we previously knew nothing about." This happens to all of us in business. However, I believe there is a far more proactive approach. I will ask my client, "In the future, could you sit in on some of your customer's advance planning meetings?" I often get that "deer in the headlights" look from my client who then says, "Yeah, you're right, we ought to go to some of their meetings." **Don't wait to communicate.**

Tip #4: Seize Opportunities for Customer Education. The other side of the coin is how well do you keep your customers informed about *what's new in your company*, who they should contact as your organization evolves, and any other "heads up" for your customers to prevent problems or save them time and money? Sometimes, you need to take the customer "behind closed doors" to let them know WHY you do things the way you do. Include them in your own advance planning whenever appropriate. The greatest organizations don't consider the customer as outside the team but rather inside the team.

A memorable quotation is: *We usually take our business where we feel more "loved."* How do customers know we truly appreciate their business and their loyalty? We stay in touch. We create opportunities to listen and to learn. We use communication to strengthen relationships. We erase any fear of the unknown by keeping them informed. And, all of these communication commitments apply to internal and external customers alike. Here's an important thought: *The longer you have been serving the customer you now serve, the less likely it is that you know what they need today.* It may be time for a good chat to be sure you are connected. **Don't wait to communicate.**

Relationship Builders

The suggestions below represent special ways to communicate your respect to your customers. The effect will be to build stronger relationships and grow your business.

- Notice and genuinely acknowledge whatever is important to your customer—in his office on the bookshelf (family photo, trophy), in the parking lot (sports sedan, luxury SUV, hybrid subcompact), etc.

- Telephone your customer occasionally for no serious reason (not just when you need something or there is a problem).

- When you read an article or book of potential interest to your customer, send her a copy.

- Be email pals. Drop your customer a quick note of helpfulness now and then. Keep it short.

- Use your customer's name often. Personalize everything you can. Put a handwritten "thank you" note inside the shipping container.

- Remember important dates/events, both personal and business. Greeting cards are magic.

- Never be late without prior notice. And, when a special occasion arises and the customer hopes you can meet at an odd hour, go out of your way to *just be there*.

- Express appreciation. While respecting each organization's ethical guidelines regarding gifts, find appropriate ways to recognize your customers for helping you to prosper.

- Ask permission to provide advice or criticism. Talk about WHAT happened, not WHO did it.

- When the customer offers criticism or advice, take it. Be grateful for it. Take notes. Thank the customer. Ask for more.

- Always be of good humor. If you trip on the customer's doormat, say, "That's interesting. I'll watch out next time."

- Make sure your doormat is fastened down so there's no way your customer will trip on it.

- Hustle. Walk briskly. Set realistic deadlines and always beat them.

- Ask the customer for any time limits at the outset of a meeting. Stick to the ending time unless permission to extend the meeting is granted.

- Stand up when your customer enters the room—male or female. Old fashioned. You bet. Just do it.

- Answer the phone slowly and calmly as if to say, "I am so glad you called," not, "Whew, am I busy, hope you don't talk too long."

- Check the accuracy of numbers on the invoice, the order form, and the proposal. Check them again.

- Explain stuff in terms familiar to the customer. Never talk over his head. Include a short "executive summary" with any document over 5 pages long.

- Don't yawn while your customer is talking.

- Don't run out of stuff your customer needs. Have a special reserve of just "two extra" of priority items the customer may suddenly need. Figure out how to reconcile this tactic with your otherwise *Just in Time* inventory strategy.

- Thank your customer often. Express appreciation for his colleagues who have supported you both.

- Take good notes about everything that is important to your customer. Always have a pen or pencil on your person. For heaven's sake, the customer may need to sign an order.

- Be cool. Make it fun and socially advantageous for your customer to be with you and to be associated with your organization. Take your customer to lunch. Take your customer to a ballgame or a concert. Take your customer to a seminar.

- Support the things your customer believes in. Partner up to serve the community.

- Be a connector. Make it easier for your customer to network with others who will support her goals.

- Read more. Travel more. Become knowledgeable for your customer's sake. He looks to you as the expert. Be one.

- Speak highly of your own organization and your associates. Your customer likes to do business with other winners.

- Use your own products and services. Provide information and education about the exciting things your organization does and how these will support your customer.

Next to your circle of family and friends, it is generally true that your work associates and your customers have the very biggest impact on the quality of your life. Make an investment in these relationships. This investment will pay off in many tangible and intangible ways that will make your life more successful and satisfying.

Secret #3

Get It Together!

Imagine asking someone for a chain to tow your car and they deliver a box of chain links—unattached chain links. As strong as the links are, it is their LINKAGE that makes them truly useful. This is also the case with your team. You may be individually competent, but it is the combined resourcefulness and the continuity of service you represent AS A TEAM that makes you truly powerful for the customer.

And, what if the *Chain of Customers* is just plain broken? The customer always knows when your Chain of Customers is broken. They recognize the underlying "we haven't got it together" message when they encounter situations such as the ones below...

Situation 1: A customer calls the accounting department about a discount their sales rep had promised them and hears, "Sorry, there's nothing in your file about this discount. Our sales people promise lots of things they never tell us about and it's a problem. I'll call your sales rep and see what she wants me to do." Actual Message: *I don't have a lot of faith in our sales people, and when they don't talk to me it makes my job even more frustrating.*

Situation 2: A customer stops an employee in the hallway to ask for assistance and hears, "I'm sorry I can't help you. I just work here." Actual Message: *I'm not really a member of the team so I don't have to do any more than I'm assigned to do.*

These situations, and many variations on these, signal to the customer that someone is a detached link—that the chain is broken.

Excuse Removal

So, what is the answer? The answer is "Team Linkage Protectors." Those who are your leaders must keep the chain intact by taking responsibility for addressing what I call your S & C factors, where S stands for *Systemic* and C stands for *Cultural*. Leaders must create and maintain an environment where *Customer Astonishment* can be a natural occurrence. This requires serious dedication to "excuse removal." While it is true that some members of your organization may lack the motivation to *astonish* their customers, most of your associates will put their best foot forward when given proper training, sufficient information, and adequate resources. However, *Systemic* and *Cultural* factors can and do legitimately get in the way.

Example: Systemic Factor

Take Situation 1 above. Sales people may be so busy that they do not believe they have time to make the notations that would help the accounting department be "up to date" on special discounts and other commitments made to customers. Perhaps there is some technology leverage that could be applied to make the job less of an encumbrance for busy sales people, such as more accessible communication links with the accounting department and/or a friendlier software tool for updating client records. This may be a *systemic* opportunity leaders need to address.

Example: Cultural Factor

Take Situation 2 above. While the individual in this scenario may just be having a bad day, it is quite possible that he or she honestly feels "left out of the loop" and does not have sufficient information or recognize the importance of "on the spot" customer problem solving. The individual may feel intimidated because they do not have answers for the things they get asked outside their own "narrow" area of responsibility. This feeling of "not being included" may be a *cultural* issue leaders need to address.

When I train the members of any organization, I insist that there always be two force vectors (think two big bold arrows) in motion toward *Customer Astonishment.* One of the arrows is labeled "Associate Training." The other is labeled "S & C Factors." These must be moving together in parallel in order for the intended result to occur. The *systems* must be "tuned up" and a *culture* of service excellence must be "under cultivation" so that your team members enter a "customer friendly environment" upon completion of their training. So, where do you begin?

Systemic Factors

What are all the systems that impact your ability to *astonish* your customers? If you are United Parcel Service, each truck is a vital system. For Visa International, computers are a matter of life and death. At Disneyland, sidewalks with handrails, non-slip steps, and crystal-clear signage are essential to assure ease of customer (guest) movement. Even the envelope in which you mail an invoice to the customer is a system. If paperwork doesn't fit neatly into the envelope, it appears that you don't know what you're doing when you order envelopes.

So, the systems question is, what do you need to do to evolve or streamline your systems to provide service to the customers that is increasingly fast, reliable, and friendly? To further illustrate, as a frequent traveler I sorely dislike noisy hotel room air conditioners that interfere with my sleep. These deliver cool air in an irritating way. I am always so pleased to discover a "whisper quiet" fan rather than one that does a wind tunnel test on my pillow. We have a gas station in our neighborhood that proclaims to have the most "fuel injector friendly" gasoline. However, at any given time, a third of the pumps have a handwritten note attached that says, "Out of Order." What good is "fuel injector friendly" gasoline if the pumps don't work? And here's the double bind: Even if the customer decides to pump gas and goes inside the food mart to buy a Coke, the poor clerk at the cash register will have an uphill battle as the now-grouchy customer complains about the pumps. It is very likely the clerk will say, "I'm sorry I can't help you with the pumps. I just work here."

Here are some categories of Systemic factors you can examine and address as appropriate...

- **Delivery Mechanisms:** Communication links, trucks, envelopes, hospital gurneys, sidewalks, keep-it-hot pizza boxes, school cafeteria lines, signage of all kinds, etc. The challenge: *Smooth the way for the customer!*

- **Data Management Methodology:** Files drawers (with color-coded file tabs?), information management software, catalogs and price lists, something as simple as name tags at a seminar or conference, etc. The challenge: *Assure easy access to up-to-the-minute information for customers and all those who serve them.*

- **Telecommunication Technology:** Automated phone systems, email protocol, and more. DHL recently conducted a telephone survey of 1,004 individuals. The number one complaint was "A lack of interaction with another human," cited by 28 percent. The challenge: *Use telecommunication technology ONLY where the benefits of efficiency for customers outweigh a real need for the human touch.*

Cultural Factors

And now, let's consider an even more complex and even more subtle topic: organizational *culture*. This is a far less tangible consideration than to examine the systems you use, but every bit as important, if not more so. Here is a definition of so-called "corporate culture."

> **Corporate Culture:** The established set of principles upon which an organization of people operates. These principles are manifest in a certain pattern of behaviors. These behaviors characterize what it is the organization stands for and how those who interact with it can expect to be treated.

It is important to note that, as you examine your organizational culture, *this is not the time to criticize what you don't like about your organization or to suggest a major overhaul of everything you do.* This is an opportunity to look from the customer's perspective and to discover the enhancements you can make to what is already in place that has already been doing an adequate job up to now. *This is the time* for each person to take ownership for creating a work environment and a customer outreach that is maximally respectful for all who are involved.

Here is an illustration of how Culture comes into play. Can you recall when an employee went out on a limb for a customer and someone else sawed the limb off by saying, "That's not your job"? Assuming that the creative employee who was trying to solve the customer's problem was not violating the law or jeopardizing the lives of other employees, it would be ideal if that second someone were found cheering on his/her fellow employee and perhaps scurrying to find a trampoline to place under the tree limb in case of an innocent mishap. So, what are the cultural implications here? Do you have a work culture that encourages creative problem solving and job sharing or one which narrowly restricts employee actions and penalizes initiative? The following questions provide thoughtful opportunities to begin a team discussion of possible "cultural" enhancements. Ask yourselves...

1. Is the day-to-day emphasis on *filling jobs* or *filling needs*? (more on this later)

2. Are we a pleasant outfit—fun to do business with?

3. Do we act without waiting to be asked when the customers' needs are obvious?

4. Is "YES" our favorite word? (used with plenty of sensibility, of course)

5. Do we each know what we need to know to run the business and to solve customer problems...without letting bureaucracy get in the way?

6. Do we use language and terminology that make people feel smart and never dumb?

7. Do we pitch in and truly support each other?

8. Is there plenty of recognition for *can-do* thinking and for finding new ways to solve customer problems?

9. Do we believe in good housekeeping? (It is indicative of the pride we take in everything else we do.)

10. Do we really listen to each other? (This is the best training for listening to our end customers.)

The Sell-Out Scenario

Considering that so much of your "culture" is about the day-to-day behaviors that characterize who you are, let's consider one final example of a broken Chain of Customers. Suppose a customer telephones you as a CSR, Customer Service Representative, to complain about an improper billing. Let's presume that you are experiencing a very hectic day and the air conditioner in your office is not working. Suppose you say this to the customer, "I'm sorry about the error. Our accounting people should have caught that. Actually, some of them are quite new and probably don't understand what's happening with your account." Yikes! In the heat of the battle, you have just sold out your accounting department and whoever hired and then failed to train them. This is not cool. It is not consistent with the culture of service excellence you are trying to cultivate and to convey to the customer.

What's the remedy to prevent the "sell-out scenario"? We are all human and prone to occasional errors, to frustration, and to forgetfulness. We need clear principles to guide us. For example, in the situation above, here is a "guiding principle" that can make a difference: *Deal with issues, not personalities.* In the situation above, apologize for the billing error if there is one. Tell the customer you will check with the accounting department and have the appropriate person follow up. (Be sure you do.) This is all you say. Remember: **Apologize for the problem or the situation but never apologize for your co-workers or the company.**

Principles of Team Conduct

It is now time for a "brown bag lunch" meeting with your team to brainstorm two lists: (a) a list of difficult or challenging situations you will face in dealing with customers (internal and external) and (b) practical principles you can agree to that will guide your behavior in these situations. We will call these, *Principles of Team Conduct*, which are meant to guide your actions as you resolve the conflicts that occur within teams and in dealing with your customers from time to time. After all, conflict is normal. It's how you handle it that makes a difference. Some teams call these principles their *Team Rules*. To illustrate, the table that follows is an example of the one you might create on a flipchart or whiteboard during your own team conversation. The table includes some of the team rules our clients have found to be especially useful. Consider these, but be sure to add those that address the unique requirements of your team and your customers.

Difficult / Challenging Situations	Principles of Team Conduct
1) When problems arise, there is a tendency to want to "pin the blame" on something or somebody. This is the "sell out" scenario.	1) **Deal with issues, not personalities.** Remember to fix the problem, not the blame.
2) When people state strong opinions, there's a tendency to overreact and become defensive.	2) **Reserve Judgment.** Before taking sides on the issues, let's be sure we understand the issues.
3) The customer seems overly distraught and impatient. The tendency is to want to move on and gloss over underlying issues.	3) **Listen with the ears of a detective and the heart of a friend.** Listen for the facts and the impacts. Ask the customer to help you understand why they feel so strongly.
4) Natural rivalries often exist among team members and among departments within an organization.	4) **Instead of EGO, how about WE-GO?**
5) There is a tendency to get in a hurry and forget to keep others informed—to not "close the loop," as they say.	5) **TTB: Touch the Bases!** Take a chapter from baseball. You can run around the ball diamond to home plate, but it doesn't count unless you "touch the bases."
6) [Keep going, as needed.]	6) [Make these simple and memorable.]

Prioritize these. Pick the Top 4 or 5 and focus on these for the next 3-6 months. As your team conquers these situations and you cultivate positive behaviors that become habits, add some additional *team rules* to the top priority list and expand your repertoire of customer interaction skills and commitments.

In conclusion, develop systematic processes and orderly procedures that make it easy for your customers to do business with you. Be sure your *Chain of Customers* is intact. Commit to those behaviors that constitute a culture of service excellence and make it easy for you to put your best foot forward to be the professionals that you are. The bottom line will be that your customers see you as a team that *has its act together*. You will be a "world-class act," in fact. I will applaud you and so will your customers.

Secret #4
Know Your Customers!

Several years ago, marketing gurus and customer care consultants announced that we had entered the age of one-to-one marketing. The age of "one size fits all" was history. I believe it. The cell phone is a perfect example of where technology has taken us. For example, you can choose the background image on the small visual display, download a few stanzas of a favorite melody as your "ring tone," create a personalized voicemail greeting, maintain your address list on a SIM card, and put that "favorite person" on speed-dial key #2. We all expect this same responsiveness from many of the other products and services we use. And, each of us knows how great it feels to visit a favorite restaurant to be greeted by name and offered a booth near that window we like so much. This is the *Age of the Customer* in terms of customization and personalized care.

Behavioral Preferences

How well do you know your customers? Let's begin by recognizing that, at a macro level, customers do manifest certain behavioral preferences that give us initial clues as to how we can better adapt and respond to them in a more personalized manner. One of my finest mentors was the late Ned Herrmann. I have had the privilege of sitting at his feet as a student and soaking up the wisdom he garnered as a senior executive at GE and as one of the world's most creative examiners of how we each choose to respond to the world around us. Based on his study of "brain dominance," we gain the following insight about customer behavior. Please study the simple grid below. Consider the four cells, counter-clockwise, from Facts through Future.

	Deliberate	Spontaneous
Rational	**FACTS**	**FUTURE**
Instinctive	**FORM**	**FEELINGS**

To summarize the insight to be gained from this table, there are customers who would almost appear to need **FACTS** for breakfast. They do not function well until you provide them a level of detailed information. These individuals think things through in an outwardly *rational* and *deliberate* way.

Then, there are those whose behavioral preferences can be characterized by the word **FORM**. They even like well-thought-out forms. These individuals are not so much some concerned with collecting *all* the facts as they are with organization and predictability. They trust their *instincts* and are very *deliberate* about orderliness and an underlying adherence to tradition.

Other *instinctive* customers have a greater need for a "hands-on, here and now" experience that is tied to that "human touch" we all recognize. Their **FEELINGS** about your products and services are very important. Hence, the familiar term we hear in this high-tech age, "Customer Friendly." It is not enough that technology is practical and useful; it must also be easy to use, even fun to use. This is where that element of *spontaneity* comes in.

Finally, those who think their way through life with an important air of creativity are preoccupied with the **FUTURE**, which means their dreams and aspirations are especially important. While taking an outwardly *rational* approach, these individuals are more spontaneous and quicker to speculate than their "facts-oriented" counterparts.

A Trip to the Auto Mall

As you consider Ned Herrmann's model for understanding behavioral preferences, you will begin to recognize your own behavioral preferences as an individual and as a customer. The insight you gain about yourself and others will help you be a better "reader of people" as you commit to adapting and personalizing your products and services to meet the unique needs of your various customers. Ask yourself, "Am I fundamentally *Facts, Form, Feelings*, or *Future*-oriented or some combination of two or three of these?" While we are each capable of operating in all four behavioral dimensions, we generally have one or two behavioral preferences and one or two lesser preferences—even an area of least preference or avoidance. Consider yours.

One of the friendliest ways I guide my seminar groups to learn the concepts of *Facts, Form, Feelings,* and *Future* is to analyze the relatively common experience of shopping for an automobile. Please imagine that you work for a small company that has finally reached the size that justifies a "company car," which will be available to you and your teammates when you must run company errands or pick up customers at the airport. Imagine that you have been assigned to be the task force leader who will select several of your teammates to join you in a visit to the local auto mall, as you pick the most appropriate vehicle to meet your company's needs. As an astute team leader, you realize the importance of a balanced and complete perspective on this decision. You recognize the unique capabilities of your teammates and select someone who is good at analyzing the details (FACTS) and another individual who will protect the core values of your company and assure an orderly process (FORM). A third member of your task force will be sure your fellow employees will like the "look and feel" of whatever car you choose (FEELINGS). The fourth member of your team will be certain the automobile you choose benefits from the latest technological enhancements and will serve you well into the FUTURE. For purposes of better understanding these four behavioral preferences, try to imagine where your four task force members will go, once they arrive at the auto mall in order to gain the information and experience each of them needs most. (Please notice the bolded key words below.)

Where will FACTS go?

Your FACTS-oriented friend will have undoubtedly done some serious research before arriving at the auto mall. However, once at the mall, she will go directly to the **window sticker** on the nearest showroom model and begin examining the **detailed specifications** of that vehicle. Then, she will move from vehicle to vehicle doing her comparative analysis. She will be particularly concerned about the **price** of each vehicle.

Where will FORM go?

The champion of FORM, orderliness, organization, and predictability will be found in the **service department** reading the **warranty manual**. He will also be found checking under the hood and kicking the tires to be sure the vehicle is well designed for maximum **reliability**.

Where will FEELINGS go?

As for the look and feel of each car, after having strolled around each vehicle to admire the exterior curves and colors, your FEELINGS partner will be found **nestled in the fine Corinthian leather** seats of one very "cool" car, with the stereo on and the speakers cranked. This person's chief concern will be that people **enjoy** driving the car—that it is comfortable and both driver and passenger-friendly.

Where will FUTURE go?

Finally, where will your FUTURE-oriented teammate be found? You look around. You search. Finally you ask the sales manager, "Have you seen my friend in the purple sweater and red sneakers?" The answer: "Oh yeah, he's on a **test drive**." I just saw him peel out of here with one of our sales people." By the way, this test drive is about **performance**.

Here comes the opportunity for that one-to-one marketing approach that says you're reading your customers. If you were the sales person at the auto mall, how would you approach each individual above? Hopefully, you would be reading the behavioral preference clues so as to not be "clue-less" and miss the opportunities to connect with and influence each unique prospect.

The ultimate purchase decision for this "staff car" will be a collective one. However, each individual will have a unique perspective that must be addressed in order to win her or his support for the team decision and thereby make the final sale. Here's the challenge: Imagine that you are the sales person who happens to be FACTS-oriented and loves to sell the deal, including the great price, low down payment, and easy payment plan. Will you approach the FEELINGS customer seated comfortably in the fine Corinthian leather driver's seat and ask him to step outside the car and come over to your desk so you can explain "the deal"? What would be the best way to relate to this customer? Answer: GET IN THE CAR, sit down, rub the fine leather seat cushion, and listen to the music. Then, LISTEN to the customer. Ask, "What do you like most about this 'cool' car? Do you have any questions?" Then, invite the customer to your desk. Aha.

With each unique customer, you can see the contrast between a real "disconnect" or the opportunity to genuinely relate to each customer's distinct needs and interests. The following table summarizes some very important characteristics of each of these customer profiles as a starting point for avoiding the "one size fits all" syndrome. Each of these characteristics will be a clue as to how to communicate and follow-through with each customer type.

	Values	Asks	Needs	Buys	Learns
FACTS	Accuracy	What?	Time	Price/Value	Documentation
FORM	Predictability	How?	Clarity	Reliability	Checklists
FEELINGS	Relationships	Who?	Participation	Enjoyment	Discussion
FUTURE	Freedom	Why?	Space	Performance	Experiments

As you interact with each customer "type" or profile, the process will certainly be enhanced and made more "personal" as you do the following, based on the five "clues" for each of the 4-F behavioral preferences...

1. Build a better customer relationship as you discover and protect the *values* of each customer.

2. Be patient with each customer's *questions* (What, How, Who, or Why) and provide relevant answers.

3. Provide what each customer *needs* in the process of working with you and making decisions about doing business with you.

4. Target your marketing and customer support at the *buying* preoccupations (Price, Reliability, Enjoyment, or Performance) of each customer.

5. Deliver information (customer education) in the mode that best fits the distinct *learning styles* of your customers.

You may ask: What if I am addressing a mixed audience of customers? Answer: You should set aside time with various segments of that audience to tailor your presentation to them or be sure to provide a smorgasbord of information, with something for everyone.

These behavioral preferences also apply when supporting your internal customers. The underlying message of these customer profiles is this: *You must be versatile to succeed in business.* Many studies have been conducted to determine which of the behavioral profiles is most likely to succeed in business and in life. No one profile is better than the other. And, inasmuch as *people like people like themselves*, you will at least succeed with those who are like you, whatever percentage that may be. HOWEVER, if you wish to be maximally successful—to be the super sales person, the true *customer astonisher*, you must be versatile, FLEXIBLE, and willing to role shift to accommodate those you serve. As you learn to relate to all four of the basic customer profiles, you will *quadruple* your success potential. That's something worth considering.

Your Immediate Family of Customers

Now, let's talk about really getting to know your particular customers—moving to the next level of knowledge about them.

First, there are your own teammates and those within your immediate organization who are your first line of support and/or responsibility. Get to know these individuals. Create mechanisms for staying in touch with them so they know your needs and you know theirs. Next, consider your own "customer base" within your particular industry or service sector. These are your "end customers." Answer these questions…

1. What are the social and professional profiles of these *end* customers (clients, members, guests, etc.)?

2. What are the age distribution, education levels, and income levels of your customers, typically? (These are so-called demographics.)

3. Where is the greatest geographic concentration of your customers?

4. What is the economic value of one of these customers, on average? (How much money does each customer typically spend on your products/services, or generate by way of membership fees, taxes, etc.?)

5. What do your customers most need from you and your associates?

6. Why do they choose to do business with you?

7. In what other ways (direct and indirect) do your customers affect your business? Where do they have influence with others who are important to your success?

8. What distinctive likes and dislikes do your customers typically have?

9. What mechanisms are in place to assure effective customer communication?

Communication mechanisms are vital. These will include periodic "customer panels," friendly feedback forms, opportunities for one-on-one conversations, access via your Website, and much more.

Priority Customers

As you come to know your customers better and better, become aware of "priority customers." This topic will beg the question: Aren't all customers important? The answer is mostly yes. Every customer deserves courtesy and professional attention. However there are, in many businesses, those who deserve special attention. The most notable industry example of "priority customers" is the concept of frequent flyers in the airline industry.

Many businesses take a customer inventory from time to time. They often discover that some customers would be better served by another supplier. Some customers are mainstay customers. Other customers are so important that every possible action must be taken to keep these customers loyal. Here is one set of criteria for determining who may be your priority customers.

Priority Customers will...

• Have a consistent and ongoing need for your products and services that translates into a very profitable business relationship over time.

• Relate to and be inclined to help you achieve your Core Purpose.

• See a distinct advantage in doing business with you—something they believe your competitors do not provide or represent.

• Support you in getting business with others, if in no other way than by *word of mouth*.

• Collaborate with you, this is, team up with you to accomplish special projects that may be of a business nature or community service related.

Up Close and Professional

Some of you reading this book provide professional services to individual clients or you represent your company in managing key accounts. When you have an ongoing relationship with key decision makers, you recognize the need to go one level higher in knowing your customers. Below are two checklists of information you may wish to gather to "go the extra mile" to signal the importance of these individuals to you and to your organization. Keep a file on each customer or include this information in your customer database.

Business Focus:

- Customer's full name

- Customer's title and professional responsibilities

- Principal products/services used

- Economic significance to you and your organization

- What this customer needs most from us

- Why this customer chooses to do business with us

- This customer's biggest concern in doing business with us

- Opportunities for *conversations* and *feedback* that we must create and encourage

- Key next steps to cement our *value added* into this customer's mind

- How we will measure progress toward continually improving the relationship

Personal Profile:

- Significant commitments and interests outside of work that may represent opportunities for collaboration and friendship

- Professional experience, formal education, and other accomplishments to acknowledge and to draw upon

- Personal "points of pride" that are keys to "what is truly important" to this customer of which we can simply be aware and acknowledge as appropriate (these include family, home, distinctive automobile, trophies, professional certifications, etc.)

- Important philosophies of business and life (favorite books are a key)

- Long range career and personal goals that we can support

- Chief worries, pressures, or special sensitivities that we can help to minimize

- Favorite restaurants, sports, cultural events, music, books, etc.

Of course, along with the above list goes the caution to not be invasive or to infringe upon personal privacy. The above list is for those of you who have built and must sustain a high degree of personal influence and trust with the key individuals who play a vital and ongoing role in your livelihoods and careers. Such information is treated with great confidentiality and its only purposes are to honor these key contacts and to strengthen the rapport you have with them in ways that are mutually beneficial.

Above all else, let your knowledge of your customers have one principal result, which is to increase your RESPECT for those who make your livelihood possible. Their concerns are legitimate. Their needs are important. Their choosing to do business with you is a matter of trust.

Secret #5
Know the Bear!

I remember: We had planned the vacation of a lifetime with our seven children. The oldest were getting ready to head off for college and we knew it would most likely be our last big adventure all together. We chose to drive our Dodge van from Utah to Alberta, Canada with our ultimate destination being the glorious region surrounding Banff. The trip would take us along the beautiful seacoast of Washington to Vancouver and then across British Columbia through Kamloops and over the Rocky Mountains and into Banff. We had plans and reservations for many fun outings: canoeing, horseback riding, glacier trekking, and more.

I have especially vivid memories of one of our outings. We loaded the family in the van and drove toward Jasper to view a spectacular glacier we had read about. When we arrived at the park headquarters, the park rangers cautioned us about going too deep into the forest as a mother Grizzly bear had been sighted with her two cubs in recent weeks. They could not be sure where she had wandered. We unloaded the van, and proceeded to hike around a small lake and through the forest to view the glacier. We figured the probability was low that we would encounter bears, if we stayed on the marked trails.

As we walked around the lake, our resolve began to weaken. As we got farther and farther away from the park headquarters, the more alone and on our own we began to feel. Sharon and I began to question the wisdom of taking our children into a region where a mother Grizzly might be tending and defending her cubs. My oldest son, Vance, and I discussed what we would do to protect the family should a bear show up on the trail ahead of us. We even discussed who would bravely sacrifice himself as a distraction should such a bear choose to attack our family. We knew our bravado was just short of stupidity, but we played the tough guys.

We finally reached a point where we could clearly see the glacier through the forest. We stopped to rest. Vance and I decided that we should go on ahead to scout the trail and determine how difficult the course would be. As we prepared to leave Sharon and the other children behind, suddenly all of my protective instincts rose to the surface and erased my bravado. I declared that our daring trek into bear country was over.

We began our hike back to the park headquarters. As we did, our joviality and sense of adventure was replaced by a quiet enjoyment of the beauty surrounding us and with a good dose of vigilance as we rounded each corner and climbed over each hill. We sang some songs. I cracked some jokes. Nevertheless, we each had one thing on our minds: a highly protective mother Grizzly with two cubs. This was certainly a bear I'd rather avoid than confront. Similarly, there are potential situations with your customers that you should prevent to be sure these do not jeopardize *your family* of valued business friends.

Only the Paranoid Survive

Andy Grove, founder and former chairman of Intel Corporation, wrote the book, *Only the Paranoid Survive*. That's a foreboding title, but it speaks volumes about the highly competitive world of business we all face each day. This is the age of Six Sigma quality and 24/7 service. What does it all mean? People ask me, "Where does *Customer Astonishment* end? Once you *astonish customers*, don't they just expect you to 'raise the bar' even higher?" The answers are: *Customer Astonishment* doesn't end and, YES, the bar will continue to be raised higher and higher. Who or what is responsible for this highly demanding business environment? We all are. Technology is. The more technology we access, the more enhancements we can make to the products we design, build, and sell. We all want the latest, greatest, and cheapest gadgets we can get. I once heard a vice president of Motorola Corporation address members of the Arizona Quality Alliance and say, "At Motorola, we have finally figured out what our customers really want." She paused and then continued, "They want perfect products, immediately, and free." Everybody in the room chuckled, but it was a nervous chuckle. We knew this was true. We all want totally reliable phones that are delivered instantly once we order our cell-phone service. And, with the right promotional offer, we expect that one or more of the phones will be "free."

Continuous Vigilance

The answer to all of this is VIGILANCE. There is a "mother Grizzly" out there and if we rest too long, she'll sneak up on us. If you think you can run fast, you must run faster. If you think you are strong, you must be stronger. To illustrate how proactive we must be, let me tell you about Ridgeview Cleaners, the neighborhood dry cleaners we have used for a number of years. The Korean-American proprietor is extremely quality-oriented and service-conscious. His employees are very friendly and so responsive to our needs. As soon as we walk through the door and before we get to the counter they push the button on the automated conveyor system to locate and retrieve our items of apparel. They have a seemingly perfect system for keeping track of our particular items. This system is probably computerized at some level, but it also includes a very personal knowledge of who we are and what we routinely have dry-cleaned or laundered. I believe they know the exact style and manufacturer of each of my sport coats and the accompanying trousers. As further assurance that we will get personalized service, we have been provided with a personalized laundry bag for use in collecting and delivering our clothing to the cleaners. They have raised the bar.

I began this chapter of the book during a business trip to Anchorage, Alaska. This morning as I prepared to leave the very comfortable Captain Cook hotel in downtown Anchorage, I was folding my shirts and placing them in the suitcase. I noticed one of the shirttails and something I couldn't remember having seen before. There was the name "Checketts" carefully written on the inside of the very tip of the shirttail. I quickly checked my other shirts. They were marked in an identical manner—every one. Wow! Ridgeview Cleaners had four levels of tracking for my particular shirts: the automated inventory/convey system, the personalized laundry bag, those familiar numeric paper tags stapled to each shirt, and *our name written on each shirttail.* I was *astonished.* There is no way they will be surprised by the bear and lose one of my shirts.

Vigilance comes in two forms: *watching for problems* and *preventing problems.* It is great when the dry cleaners employees watch for my shirts and are aware of potential opportunities to lose a shirt. It is even more *astonishing* when they have put in place failsafe mechanisms to be sure my shirts won't get lost. It is important to note that nearly any investment you make in these failsafe mechanisms will be returned to you many times as you avoid the back peddling, embarrassment, apologies, corrective actions, and loss of goodwill that comes from not having such systems.

Beware the Morphing Bears

What forms do these *bears* take? Heaven forbid that your customers encounter the bears called "incompetence" or "negligence." These are especially ferocious. The more obvious forms bears take are *poor quality* and *substandard service.* These bears would be large, loud, and standing upright on the trail in front of your customers. Then, there are those sneaky, hidden-in-the-forest bears that are an equally serious threat. These come in different forms: *failure to have contingency plans* and *letting your competitive edge grow dull.* The very best customer care teams always have Plan B to accompany Plan A so that they can minimize unpleasant surprises for the customer. Great customer care teams also sharpen their competitive edge on a regular basis through continuous education and technology updating. If you fall behind on these commitments, the bear will gain on you and frighten your customers. You will all wish you had been faithfully attending the gym and that you were wearing top-notch running shoes as you now try to outrun the bear. Otherwise, it's too late.

Know the bears. Know your vulnerabilities. Know your competition. Know what's changing in your industry and marketplace. Be vigilant. Know what it takes to outrun the bears. Consider the following guidelines to evaluate your products and services. Be sure you are vigilant about **BVPD**: Beauty, Value, Precision, and Dependability. From a customer's perspective, consider the products and services that *you* purchase and appreciate. Have you ever caressed the handle of a new tennis racquet or fishing pole and been both delighted and *astonished*? You were experiencing **BVPD**. As you have enjoyed a delicious meal and impeccable service at your favorite restaurant, you have experienced **BVPD**.

Beauty, Value, Precision, and Dependability

Beauty. Is your product beautiful—beautiful to look at, which can take the form of a shiny, curvaceous automobile or a super-efficient, shaped-for-the-hand chef's spatula? Some product/marketing analysts report that competition among products 30 years ago centered on *cost*. Competition among products 10-15 years ago centered on *quality*. In today's competitive marketplace, fair price and high quality are assumed to be the case and taken for granted. Product competition in today's marketplace centers on *design*. Is your product attractive, color-coordinated, smooth-to-the-touch, conveniently shaped to fit on a desk or on the kitchen counter, and so on?

Value. Does your product or service represent a "good deal"? Is it an unquestionably good investment of the customer's time and money? Is the customer better off because of your product or service?

Precision. Did somebody who is really smart figure out how the product would be designed and assembled? If the customer should have to assemble it himself, is it guaranteed that all the necessary nuts and bolts are included in the plastic bag inside the box? Take a few minutes to look closely at the gear-shifting mechanism on a quality bicycle. The many component parts are a joy to behold, so carefully designed and manufactured—all meshing and working together perfectly. Quite an accomplishment! Similarly, well-designed administrative procedures represent "precision." For example we all know the difference between easy-to-understand forms with readable print and plenty of space for the required information and those hellish forms that are poorly designed. Next time you check in for a flight at the airport, notice the security inspection procedures. They differ from airport to airport. Some of those TSA (Transportation Security Administration) folks are tired and bogged down. Others are clever and cheerful. We appreciate their precision.

Dependability. Years ago the Timex Company staked the reputation of its wrist watches on the slogan, "It takes a licking and keeps on ticking." We all value such reliable, durable, and long-lasting products. I now use a Seiko kinetic watch that is quite old, never skips a beat, and never needs a battery change. It's just there on my left wrist forever doing its job. Amazing. Will your product be trouble free over an extended period of time? Will your customers always proclaim that you delivered what you promised? We live in an age when any product hassle is cause for choosing your competitor's product next time. The bear is only allowed to show up just so many times before we run to the competition.

Be Customer Champions

The message is: Keep all bears at a far distance from your customers through constant vigilance. Be a true Customer Champion. Here is the Customer Champion's Creed...

1. **Make prior planning a top priority**. Be eager to learn what is "coming down the road" for the customer. Provide multiple options for problem solving and minimize surprises for everyone, except on their birthdays.

2. **Smooth the way for the customer**. Consistently practice the **A-R-T** of systems management. Guarantee the availability of *Adequate* resources that are fully *Responsive* to customer needs and *Technologically* up to date.

3. **Be sure everybody wins.** As true customer champions, be sure your fundamental goals are to satisfy customer needs, to exceed expectations, and to equitably support the interests of all key individuals who are your partners in success. Keep everybody *informed and secure* in the knowledge that the bears are far away in their forest habitat where they belong.

Red Alert

If you ever notice that the buying habits, the frequency of communication, or any other significant behaviors begin to deviate from the customer's typical pattern of doing business with you, you could be in the process of losing a customer. A Grizzly bear could be nearby. Calmly contact the customer to learn what has changed. Take decisive corrective and preventive action. You cannot, *you simply cannot afford to lose a good customer*. It does take three to five times the investment of time and money to find a new customer as it does to keep an existing one. Vigilance is the key. Take rightful pride in keeping your competitive edge sharp.

Secret #6

Take Ownership!

There's a great truism that certainly applies to customer care: *A drowning person cannot save another drowning person.* Have you had swimming lessons?

Imagine that a frazzled customer calls to express frustration and the CSR responds with "Hey, I'm having a bad day, too. What can you do for me?" I remember talking to a group of retail clerks in one department store who told me: "We're fed up with grouchy customers. These customers should be grateful there's a store here for them to shop in and they should treat our store employees with more respect." From time to time, I will have someone in a seminar audience ask me if there is a course available for difficult customers. Can you imagine calling one of your grouchy customers and telling them they must attend the "How to Be a Nice Customer" seminar before they can do business with you? Whether or not we like the reality, the shoe is on your foot or mine and not on the customer's. We are at their service, not the other way around.

A World Class Swimmer

A few years ago, after a long transatlantic flight, I found myself standing at the registration desk of the Copthorne Hotel in Birmingham, England. I was second in line behind a man who I soon and ashamedly discovered was a "fellow" American. He was berating the young Englishwoman on the other side of the desk—

demanding one thing and another in the harshest of tones. She responded with, "I apologize for that situation, Sir. I will look into it straightaway and call you in your room in about 20 minutes. Will that be okay?" She handled one concern after another with patience and objectivity. As he took his key and stormed off to the elevators, I remarked to the hotel clerk that her performance was "so professional," especially in the face of a man who was, quite frankly, acting like a total jerk. She thanked me and said these immortal words as we continued a brief chat…

> *Mr. Checketts, thank you for your kind remarks about my service. Actually, it can get a little boring standing here, hour after hour, saying, "Here are your keys and there are the elevators." When one of those customers comes along, I get to find out just how good I really am. You see, a computer can register a happy customer; it takes a professional to handle a difficult one. I'm not going to let a customer turn around my attitude. By tomorrow morning, I hope to have helped that gentleman turn around his attitude, with most of his problems resolved and a much better outlook.*

Wow! That's all I could say. I thought to myself how valuable a few hundred of her clones would be across the Atlantic at numerous other hotels I visited.

The Greatest Secret of the Ages

At the heart of dealing effectively with the world of work and with your customers is the rediscovery of the *greatest secret of the ages*: **You create your world by how you *think* and *speak* about it.** There is never just one world, there outside your window (or standing across from you at the hotel check-in counter). There's whatever world you think it is. One person looks outside the window at the world, sees rain clouds and says, "Oh no, it's going to rain. Our picnic plans will be ruined." Another person sees rain clouds and says, "Hooray, it's going to rain. Our garden will be saved." The person thinking about picnics sees one world. The person thinking about gardens sees another. The rain is just there, that's all. It is a reality. All the thinking or speaking about the rain isn't going to change anything *about the rain*. However, your thinking and speaking can change *your* world. And, here's what's really amazing about life. You can change your thoughts and change your world as quickly and as easily as you can push different buttons on your TV's remote control to change what you see and what you experience in your family room or den. Ultimately, you can transform the outcome of situations you face in business and in life by recognizing two fundamental thinking channels or systems and then by choosing the one that works best.

Two Systems: Owner...Victim

The two powerful thinking channels or systems we can access with our mental channel changers are the **Owner** system and the **Victim** system. The person accessing the *owner* system takes responsibility for situations and outcomes. The person accessing the *victim* system simply figures that "stuff happens and you must struggle through it somehow." The young woman at the Copthorne Hotel could have become a "victim of" her grouchy customer. Instead, she defined the situation as an opportunity to demonstrate her truest professionalism.

To further contrast these systems, consider the "owner" person who is busy *getting from* life all that she or he can in terms of learning, strength, experience, excitement, and more. Conversely, the "victim" person is focused on just *getting through* the week to have some "free time" on the weekend *or* "getting through those teenage years with our kids" *or* somehow getting through to retirement *or* just getting through the next phone call with a customer. The happiness of life is always "out there" somewhere hopefully waiting for the beleaguered person to get through whatever's getting in the way at the moment. And, it is the moment at hand that holds the only real promise for happiness there is. The "owner" will seize that moment and create the world around it.

Perhaps the most powerful Owner-Victim contrast is about *commitment*. Once upon a time, it was said that the saddest phrase of tongue or pen was, "It might have been." Today, I think the saddest phrase of tongue (or word processor) is, "I'm sort of committed." Why? It is technically impossible to be "sort of committed." In the Victim system, commitment is just *a feeling*. In the Owner system, commitment is *a decision*. What does it mean when someone says, "You know, our company is just not the same company it was five or 10 years ago"? I'm not feeling as committed as I used to." That's the language of "feeling" discouraged, disconnected, and NOT committed. The owner mentality goes like this, "The business has changed, but as long as I choose to butter my bread here, this must be the best darned company in town."

Consider this about where you work. If you "feel" it is a dumb place to work, why would you work there much longer? Okay, if it's the only job you could possibly qualify for in the entire free world, I understand. Or, if you are three hours and 27 minutes away from cashing in on a fantastic retirement program, I understand. Otherwise, I would question why a smart person would work for a dumb company when there are plenty of smart companies out there. You are either committed to your work or not. What you feel about your work is something else. The owner grabs the channel changer and begins to deal with whatever the obstacles may be—to remove these or navigate around them. The owner loves what is. The owner wastes no time in self-pity.

There is a companion concept to accompany "ownership." It is "stewardship." You see, once someone discovers the ownership spirit, such an individual accepts responsibility for the work, the problems, the relationships, the opportunities, and all that life has sent in his or her direction. Ownership on the inside leads naturally to stewardship on the outside. As you take control of your thoughts, you take control of situations. Customers know when you are in the "victim" mode and they see you as uncaring and unprofessional. When they see you in the "owner" mode, they want to work with you to find solutions and to get the business done with a mutually beneficial outcome.

I Am The One!

In Secret #7, we will discuss what I call *Pride Factors*. These are your own "Hallmarks of Professionalism." One of my favorite

Pride Factors that speaks of ownership came from an employee of Arizona Public Service. He said, "One of my Pride Factors is *I am the one*." He explained his customer commitment this way.

> *When a customer calls me, that customer considers me to be "the company" and their personal representative from the company. I must accept this responsibility. As I proceed to find solutions and address the customer's needs, I must be the one to coordinate with others. I am the one who must be sure the job gets done at the end of the day. And, I am the one who must "close the loop" by checking with the customer to be sure we have met their needs and exceeded their expectations. You see, **I am the one.***

The Owner takes responsibility for what life gives. If it gives him joy, he celebrates. If it gives her challenges, she creates. There are those who wait for better circumstances and those who create the circumstances they need to succeed. There are those who see customers as "more work" and those who see customers as "more opportunity." Grab your channel changer. Push the button that says "Owner." This channel will make it much easier to turn all of your customer interactions into opportunities—opportunities to learn, to help, to grow, to excel, and to prosper.

Secret #7
Stake Your Reputation!

To "stake a mining claim," you must identify the boundaries of the area you claim. To stake your reputation, you must identify the extent of your commitments. In the context of *Customer Astonishment*, we will do this by identifying crucial situations where your commitments will be especially important. We will call these situations "Moments of Truth." We will call the commitments you make as to how you will handle these situations your "Pride Factors. These Pride Factors are not about arrogance, but about personal excellence as you take pride in your work and care for your customers.

A Customer Astonishment Odyssey

Where did the concept of Pride Factors come from? Several years ago, I conducted a public seminar on *Customer Service* in Portland, Oregon. Two managers from Intel were in the room and later asked me to customize some training for their teams, which I was eager to do. This proved to be the beginning of a very important client relationship with Intel. From this and other key client relationships emerged the commitment to build a unique set of conceptual models for moving beyond traditional *customer service* to something more energizing and creative. I decided to write one and then two books on the subject (this is now the fourth). As an important part of my early research, I embarked on an eight-state odyssey with my then teenage son, Ken. Our goal was to travel from town to town and city to city to spontaneously visit companies, government agencies, schools, and other organizations. We would interview their employees and learn what key factors prompted them to "take pride in their work" or not. During these fascinating interviews, we identified various *Pride Killers* and we discovered certain *Pride Builders*. (Please see the Appendix for more information on these.) Everybody we met said they *intended* to take pride in their work and to care for their customers. Nobody proclaimed otherwise. We learned that the individuals we interviewed each had their own approach to taking pride in their work. We will call these commitments *Pride Factors*. Again, these are not about arrogance, but about excellence.

Individual Pride Factors usually originated in one of two ways: (a) as a result of some "childhood teachings," which the person had received or (b) in response to "specific customer situations" he or she had encountered in the course of doing business.

Childhood Teachings: These went along the following lines. "My mother *always* taught me to be honest" or "My grandfather taught me to *always* finish any job you start" or "When I was a newspaper boy 20 years ago, I learned to *always* treat my customers with respect." The word "always" occurred often as a subtle indication of an especially serious commitment to some key principle or behavior. It is interesting that "always" is measurable. You either do it or you don't.

Specific Customer Situations: These were about *Moments of Truth* individuals had encountered. Let me further illustrate. As my son and I were beginning to grasp the various factors that influence pride of workmanship and genuine customer care, we began to very actively look for examples at every turn in the road. I remember the day we turned south into the State of Kansas toward Wichita where we hoped to interview employees of the Coleman Company and Beech Aircraft. Our visits to these fine companies ultimately provided some of the most useful and most positive examples of worker pride. But, before these important visits could happen, we needed to have lunch.

It was at one small roadside café in Wichita, Kansas, that the neon lights in my mind began to flash and we crystallized the core concept of *Pride Factors* and the terminology for teaching this especially important element of *Customer Astonishment.*

The Cherry Tomato

We entered the café and the hostess directed us to our table. We examined the menu and then we each ordered a sandwich with a side salad. Several minutes later, the salads arrived. I slid my bowl closer to examine its contents. There was mostly iceberg lettuce, some shreds of carrot, and slices of cucumber. On top of the greenery was a plump, red cherry tomato. The tomato was the crowning feature and most appetizing element of the salad for me. My only wish was that there were six or seven cherry tomatoes. I smacked my lips, poured on some ranch dressing, picked up my fork and stuck it into the tomato. Oops. That fork went into the tomato a little too easily. My instincts suggested that the tomato may be overripe and I certainly prefer those crisp, go-pop-in-your-mouth cherry tomatoes instead. I ignored my instincts and put the tomato in my mouth. Ooh, ugh, yuck, disgusting. The tomato was more than overripe; it was spoiled and should have been put down the garbage disposal. I instantly lost my appetite for the salad and for everything else on the menu. I began to poke around in the salad to see what else might be lurking there that I would not want to put in my mouth.

Here is the GIGANTIC lesson from a simple, little cherry tomato. The restaurant's entire reputation was put to the test in one immensely important instant. And, they had only one opportunity to make a first impression. That Moment of Truth would signal so much about their level of product quality and customer care. If the tomato was crispy and juicy, I would eventually leave the café with a very positive attitude and recommend it to others. If not, I would be suspicious of their products and services and they would be sent into "damage control and recovery" mode. I would have been forgiving of a piece of iceberg lettuce with brownish-red edges. But, this was the crown jewel of my salad—the cherry tomato!

The Moment of Truth was *that moment* when I pushed the fork into the tomato, raised it to my mouth, and bit down. In response to this impending situation, the salad chef needed this Pride Factor: *No mooshy cherry tomatoes will show up on salads during my watch.* This would have been the *astonishing* contribution of the salad department and, as little a thing as it may seem to some, it was of GIGANTIC importance in winning my approval and my loyalty as a customer. If I were the salad chef, I would sample each new batch of cherry tomatoes personally. I would sooner throw an entire box of cherry tomatoes on the rubbish heap than have even a few bad tomatoes show up on salads. If the cherry tomatoes had to be discarded, radish slices or olives could have been used in their place, with a more positive result. And, whatever the cost of the discarded tomatoes, it would have been less than the cost of losing me as a customer. They can be thankful I am not sharing the name of their café or you would drive right on by next time you're in Wichita.

Your Pride Factors

The simplest way for me to expand on this concept is to now ask you: Where and when are your *cherry tomato moments* and what are you going to do about these to be sure your customers are *astonished* and not astounded? The situations you identify are your "Moments of Truth." **Your commitments to handling these situations well constitute your "Pride Factors."** I challenge individuals and teams to come up with three to five of these to work on for a period of six months and beyond. As you get better and better at keeping your commitments, raise the bar. Intensify your commitments and expand the number of Pride Factors.

I will soon provide a list of *Pride Factor* examples to guide you. First, let me point out that Pride Factors are not like "Core Values." Values are *philosophical.* Pride Factors are *behavioral.* The best Pride Factors meet the following criteria. They are...

1. In response to specific customer situations,

2. Often the result of customer feedback about likes and dislikes; prior disappointments and future expectations,

3. Behavioral in that you can see, hear, smell, feel what has been done to make the customer experience more positive,

4. Measurable so you can track your progress at being more aggressive about your commitments and improving your performance over time,

5. A set of stakes you drive in the ground to mark your claim to service excellence. And, these commitments are about "always," which means they are met consistently and never left to chance.

Here are some further illustrations of Pride Factors *in operation.*

TGI Friday's

I once interviewed the manager of a TGI Friday's restaurant who explained this Pride Factor: "Once a month, I sit in every seat in the restaurant." He went on to explain why he did this. "I want to know what each customer sees, feels, hears, and smells from each particular seat. I want to know if a plant leaf is blocking the view or the chair is too near the high-traffic kitchen entrance or the air conditioning is too cold or the music speakers blare too loudly overhead or the chair is wobbly and needs replacing." Wow! That's world-class customer care. And, you can see how it meets the five criteria above.

State Image Enhancers

A few years ago, I worked with the grounds keepers at the Utah State Capitol building in Salt Lake City. One of their stated Pride Factors was: "We do not water parked cars." At first, this statement draws a chuckle from those who hear it. It is funny— funny and serious and a genuine commitment. What's the Moment of Truth? Imagine that you come to visit the governor of Utah and park your shiny new, black Chevy pick-up out front. When you return from your meeting, the sprinklers have come on and there are hard water spots all over your precious truck. You do not say under your breath, "Stupid grounds keepers." You say, "Stupid State of Utah." By the way, this group of grounds keepers had also worked with me during our training session to rename what they do. They moved from a JOB title of "Grounds Keepers" that is about *things* and *processes* to a new COR title that is about *people* and *results*. They renamed themselves "State Image Enhancers." And, there is no way this group of State Image Enhancers is going to water your Chevy pick-up and then have you blame it on their state government. In case you're wondering, COR stands for "Customer Outcome Responsibility." And, JOB stands for "Just Ordinary Business." JOB is about "filling a job." COR is about "filling needs." Your COR title goes hand-in-hand with your Pride Factors.

Information Services: Eye of the Hurricane

I work with many Information Services departments inside large and some smaller organizations. These "IS" departments often represent the epitome of the "internal customer care challenge." When something goes wrong, it seems everybody wants to blame it on some information system failure—something with the computers, the software, the communication networks, the company Website, etc. When the problem is truly significant, the IS department often finds itself in the eye of the hurricane. One of the courageous Pride Factors that usually emerges is about "response time." For example: "We respond to all customer problems with a fix or a plan within two hours." Some employees will wonder if two hours is too aggressive. Customers will want the response to be immediate. Notice that this aggressive time commitment is actually based on a realistic outcome. It does not say that there will always be a "fix" within two hours. Sometimes, it will be a clear "plan to fix" so, at least, the customer will not be kept waiting in the dark wondering what the response will be. By the way, if you work in the IS department and think two hours is unrealistic, start with four hours. Once you can do four hours, raise the bar to two hours and then to one hour and then to "instantaneous" as you develop new and better tools, such as, instantaneously downloadable solutions available at your Website.

Team Pride Factors

Imagine the impact of all the members of your team each working on three to five specific commitments to their particular customers. These commitments need to be individually generated (from the heart) and not legislated. As you find you have certain Pride Factors in common, these can become your *Team Pride Factors* and will represent a friendly way to cultivate your *culture of service excellence* and to orient new employees to "who you are as a team and how you do business with those you serve." As you and your team begin to identify your Moments of Truth and then commit to your Pride Factors, here is a generic list of examples to consider.

Business Type	Moment of Truth	Pride Factor
Retail	A customer rushes to the entrance of a retail store right at closing time.	"If we're in the store and still visible to you, we're open for you."
Restaurant	As a customer awaits a great meal, she picks up a glass to examine it.	"Our spot-free reputation begins with spot-free glasses."
Government Agency	The customer is handed a form to fill out.	A completely filled-out example is provided for reference.
Medical Center	A customer arrives and expects a long wait to see a doctor.	Appointment times are realistic. "Surprise, the wait is not long."
Automobile Service	The customer gives a vivid and detailed description to the service writer.	The customer's exact words are written down without editing.
Computer Software	A thick manual is handed to the busy customer.	The customer is directed to the two-page "Quick Start" guide available in print and online.
Heavy Manufacturing	A large piece of complex equipment is delivered to the customer's plant site.	The *Installation Engineer* has been on site for two days and everything's ready.
Employee Benefits Department	An anxious parent inquires about medical coverage for a son.	"Yes, young Robert's x-rays are covered." (The child's name is known and used.)
Legal Department	A legal document is presented to the client for review.	Always included is a one to two-page summary without legalese.
Engineering Department	A project plan is submitted to the Executive Committee.	The people in Manufacturing have been "on board" from day one.
Customer Call Center (Inbound)	The phone rings.	"We give a complete greeting and 'listen actively' before making recommendations."

True Professionals

During my *Customer Astonishment* workshops, I interact with participants in the following way. Imagine that you're sitting there in the audience as we discuss the importance of Pride Factors.

What if I asked each of you, are you a professional? Nearly all of you would reply with a strong affirmation. Then, I would ask, how would I know? Quite frankly, most people struggle for a few moments to find an answer. They may mention a certificate hanging on the wall of their cubicle or proudly display their "power tie" or point to a product they manufacture. I then suggest that once you have your Pride Factors *in place, the answer is easy. You will have a list of three to five behaviors that clearly demonstrate just how professional you are.*

Now, let me ask you, can a person be perfect? The answer is generally, "No way." My response: Yes, a person, including each one of you, can be perfect. You can be perfect at something. Some of you in the room have a perfect work attendance record. Others check their spreadsheets for errors six times. Some of you are ALWAYS friendly on the phone. Others consistently include an "executive summary" with any important document you create. Congratulations, you are perfect or nearly perfect in these commitments. So, stake your reputation.

Your Pride Factors are about being the best versions of who you are as you take pride in what you do and as you positively *astonish* those you serve.

Secret #8

Add Value at Each Step of the Way!

Imagine that you and a special guest are about to try a new Italian restaurant that has just opened in your neighborhood. They have advertised their exceptional menu of "old world" Italian delights. You drive to the restaurant, park your car, enter, and wait briefly for the host to seat you. The host appears and hands you and your guest a set of plastic eating utensils wrapped in a paper napkin. He then explains that you can look around the restaurant to find a table you like, seat yourselves, and then set the table with the "dinnerware" he has provided. And, if you wish, you can stop by the kitchen to get some paper cups and ice water. He further explains that when your meal is ready, a small green light on your table will be illuminated to signal that it is time for you to go to the kitchen and pick up the food you've ordered. You are astounded and ask what this sort of "non-service" is all about. The host explains that their food is so fine and requires the use of so many special ingredients that the only way they can keep their prices at a reasonable level is to ask their guests to pitch in and help out with certain duties that servers otherwise would provide. Of course, any servers would have expected to be tipped. So, there are savings all around—for you and for the restaurant.

Well, you know where you can go to get paper napkins and plastic utensils—a fast food restaurant. You also know where you can get darned good Italian food—at home. You cook great lasagna and other dishes your mother taught you to prepare. So, why did you go to the restaurant in the first place? It was only partially about the food. It was as much about all the other value the restaurant adds to the dining experience. You expect the restaurant staff to add this value in terms of *labor savings, an intimate atmosphere for great conversation, some really nice linen napkins, and the simple pleasure of being waited upon by someone else.* Thus, you justify paying more for your restaurant meal because *it's not just about the food.*

In this Secret #8 and in Secret #9, we will be looking, scanning, envisioning, and putting in place all those "special touches" that represent your Pride Factors and signal how much you care about your customers. Consider that there are three dispositions you could have toward your customers...

1. **To Be Process Driven:** This means that you have a certain process you follow in doing business with your customers. This process is important because it is the basis for fundamental quality control and consistency.

2. **To Be Customer Driven:** This would mean that you are ready to follow any and all orders the customer might give you. This appears to be maximum responsiveness—doesn't it?

3. **To Be Customer-Need Driven:** This is to focus on the customer's particular problem, want, need, or expectation and *to deliver*—to take responsibility for the outcomes that would be most useful and *astonishing* to the customer.

Customer-Need Driven

To differentiate among these three dispositions, it is important to examine the potential liabilities of each one. If you are *Process Driven*, it is too easy to "fall in love with" your own procedures and ways of doing things and to become bureaucratic. You may end up giving the customer orders. The problem with being *Customer Driven* is that the customer is not always *exactly* right. You could be directed by the customer to do something that is ultimately not in their best interest or yours. To be *Customer-Need Driven* is the answer. In this case, it's not about YOU telling the customer what to do or the CUSTOMER telling you what to do; it's about teaming up with the customer to focus on the problem or need and to solve and address it together. The only potential liability would be that you take shortcuts with the problem analysis and your solutions miss the target. The answer is to LISTEN so that you and your customer-partner focus your combined energies on creating the most relevant outcomes.

If you are *Customer-Need Driven*, you will see more opportunities for "value added" and you will certainly be more inclined to "smooth the way" (see Secret #9). And, your "process" will be designed with the customer in mind. Here are some examples of adding value that also illustrate the power of being *customer-need driven*.

Camelot Cookies

When we moved to our current home several years ago, I had an immediate need to find someone to cut my hair. I had long since given up on the "cut and shear" barbers and preferred "hair stylists" with a little more finesse. So, I experimented by visiting several hair salons. Each of these produced a good haircut. So, how was I to choose a favorite salon? My final visit revealed the answer: chocolate chip cookies. I paid a visit to the Camelot Beauty Salon at Recker Road and McKellips Road in northeast Mesa, Arizona. As I entered, I noticed the usual three or four women cutting the hair of mostly women customers. But, two things were different. Inside the front door was a small table with chocolate chip cookies. Now, that is value added. Then, I sat down to wait my turn and noticed several "guy magazines" in the magazine rack including *Esquire* and *Road & Track*. Wow! There were alternatives to *Vogue* and *Elle*.

I later asked the owner, Irene, how she came to have "guy magazines." She told me that her husband, who is her business partner, had recommended these. At first she had been puzzled and explained to him that she didn't have very many male customers. (Do we wonder why?) He smiled patiently and asked that she trust his suggestions to add the cookies and special magazines to see what happened as she provided some new and unique "value" of interest to men. Today, Camelot has at least one more very loyal male customer—me. And, I've sent hundreds of potential customers their way looking for more than just haircuts. Some go to check out the cookies. Some stay and eat them as they wait for their first haircut or perm at the friendly new salon they've now discovered.

Paper of the Day

I heard the vice president of a major hotel chain explain how several years ago, his company decided to raise the bar for "value added" in terms of not only giving their guests a copy of the morning newspaper but giving them a choice of the local paper, the *Wall Street Journal* or *USA Today*. (This example also illustrates that adding value and being customer-need driven does not necessarily represent much added cost or effort.)

As the hotel executive began to examine what would be required to give guests these newspaper options, he asked one of his hotel managers what he thought would be involved in making such a change. This manager explained that the process would be quite involved. It would certainly require some changes to the online guest registration template to allow a place for indicating newspaper preferences. This would also mean some additional training for the front desk clerks. When asked what the cost would be per hotel, this manager guessed about $6-10,000.

A second hotel manager was asked what he thought would be involved. His reply was, "Oh, not much at all. We already do this." He explained that some months ago his local newspaper vendor had offered to provide multiple newspapers. This hotel manager quickly created a simple three-column form with three headings: Local, WSJ, and USA. Each clerk had a copy of the form at his or her check-in station. As guests would check in, the clerk would ask which newspaper was preferred and write that person's room number in the column under that heading. Easy, no software rewrite, no special training required. At the end of the evening, the tally sheets were given to the newspaper vendor who then made sure each guest's preferred paper was waiting outside the door the next morning. Simple value added, simply executed. Congratulations!

A Genuine Real Estate Professional

When we bought our home in Mesa, Arizona, we benefited from the services of the local ERA real estate office. We were living out of state when we bought the home so we were unable to attend to many of the details involved in the transaction. Our Realtor was very much a go-the-extra-mile person. She routinely coordinated many things, including the home inspection. The inspector mentioned to her that there was a plant bed just outside the master bedroom where too much dirt had been added and was piled up above the foundation level against the stucco wall. He indicated that this could cause water to seep into the wood frame inside the wall and encourage termites to nest. Our Realtor called and explained the situation to me. As I was about to ask for recommended actions, she told me that she had just put on a pair of overalls and had taken her shovel and wheel barrow to our new home to move the dirt away from the wall so the inspector could return and check for termites. Quite frankly, I would never have expected this always-neatly-attired, middle-aged woman to go "move dirt." I was *astonished* by her initiative and by her willingness to "get her hands dirty" to get the job done, whatever it took.

We soon experienced another example of her *astonishing* commitment. When we arrived in Mesa to take possession of the home and move in, we were greeted at the door by our gracious Realtor who had placed a beautiful beverage, fruit, and nut basket near the entry way. She handed us the house keys, thanked us for doing business with ERA, and left us to enjoy our new home. All these courtesies we actually expected, including the beverage, fruit, and nuts or an equivalent "thank you" gesture. However, what we did not expect was to come in from a hot Arizona afternoon after a long drive; *tired and hungry*, to open the refrigerator in the kitchen and find it completely full. There was a large cooked ham, a watermelon, an assortment of fruit juices, a beautiful salad ready to eat, a selection of breads, and much more. In the freezer, there was an assortment of ice creams (including chocolate), along with frozen vegetables and too many other creative food items to recall. Several hundred dollars worth of groceries were in our refrigerator/freezer that had to represent several hours of shopping at the local market. We were *astonished*! The perceived value of "our Realtor's" services jumped dramatically. What a fantastic impression this outstanding professional made on each member of our family.

Going the Extra Mile

The bottom line is this: *Customer-Need-Driven* professionals naturally recognize opportunities to add value and they do it. Those less experienced and who are working to cultivate such instincts simply need to start by asking this simple question: "Is there anything else I can do for you today?" At first, you will be *Responding*. As your experience with more and more customers teaches you what is possible and you build a repertoire of great ways to "go the extra mile," you will find yourself *Anticipating* opportunities for value added. Some of these opportunities will prompt your own complimentary gestures toward building customer loyalty. And, many of these gestures will be a factor for *Expanding* the prospects for more business with your customers. You'll know the difference. It's not about "freebies;" it's about *generosity in the present* and *opening the door for more business in the future*. Remember the old English saying about not being "penny wise and a pound foolish." The pennies you may carefully choose to spend for "customer extras" will lead to pounds (as in £'s) of future business.

Here's one more fun example that I promised Shon Foster I would include after he and his staff provided Sharon and me with the most *astonishing* meal. We were recently traveling through scenic southern Utah and came to the beautiful city of Kanab. We have been to Kanab before, but hoped to find a fun, new place to have lunch. We found the Rewind Café at 18 East Center Street. It is a nostalgic little café with the black, white, and red motif of a typical 1950s diner. Spencer waited on us. He introduced us to the owner, Shon Foster.

I prefer vegetarian meals and quickly noticed many such items on the menu, including their most delicious "Philly Cheese Steak Sandwich" available with "Tempeh," a product of the White Wave Company, which is famous for their soy-based milk replacement called *Silk*. Tempeh is comprised of nuts and other delicious ingredients, which take the place of beef or chicken, very admirably and healthfully so. To reassure any hearty beefeaters reading this book, the Philly Cheese Steak Sandwich is available with USDA Grade-A Rib Eye Steak as well. The Rewind team proceeded to smooth the way and add value to our dining experience in one way and then another and then another. Not only did they satisfy my quest for tasty vegetarian food, but also on the table top next to the pepper shaker there was a bottle of natural sea salt and a bottle of Salad Sprinkles—yummy extras. Also on the table was a bottle of *Germ-X* hand sanitizer. Now, a trip to the restroom to wash my hands before eating was not needed. Spencer and Shon took the time to explain various items on the menu and to give us free samples. We asked about the delicious *Shitake and Sesame Vinaigrette* salad dressing from a company called Annie's Naturals. Shon told us where to buy it and the Tempeh.

Rewind has been in business for a year. It is *the place* to have lunch in southern Utah. Please go there. Shon went on to tell us how hard he works to understand and to practice the principles of business effectiveness and *customer astonishment*. He mentioned one of his favorite books, *The E-Myth*, by Michael Gerber. By the way, the selection of 50s background music at the Rewind Café is worth the stop all by itself.

Put those FINISHING TOUCHES on the work you do for your customers. There will be a significant return on this investment as they spread the word about your linen napkins, chocolate chip cookies, the "newspaper of the day," your professionalism, your generosity, and even the Germ-X on the restaurant table. Most customers will be generous in return and sing your praises to others who will become your customers. This word-of-mouth marketing will be more powerful than any mass-marketing campaign you could ever consider and which may waste your money.

As you conclude this chapter, plan to do this simple exercise with your team. Write down the steps of the process you follow in serving and *astonishing* your customers. At each step of the way, simply ask yourselves how you could add some value that is affordable, that makes sense, and will delight your customers in ways that bring them back again and again.

Steps in the Process	Value We Can Add
Step 1	
Step 2	
Step 3	
Step 4	
Step 5	

Invest in Your Own "Value Added."

Finally, let me recommend two books about fine-tuning your business processes and choosing strategies that will truly add value for your customers and for you in turn. If you are a small business operator, read *9 Lies That Are Holding Your Business Back* by two of my great friends and partners, Steve Chandler and Sam Beckford. If you are a large business operator, read *Execution: The Discipline of Getting Things Done* by Larry Bossidy and Ram Charan. If you operate a small business and intend that it becomes a bigger business, read both books. If you are large business operator and don't want to lose your entrepreneurial edge, read both books.

Adding value is also about adding value to your own skill repertoire and that of your employees. Investing in books and studying these together is a phenomenally cost-effective way to do this.

Secret #9
Smooth the Way!

To be "Anticipatory" in addressing customer needs is to smooth the way. It means you "look out" for the customer to remove obstacles and inconveniences. This is different than being vigilant about "the bear." The bear represents those major problems with product quality or service performance that could undo your business. Smoothing the way is an extension of customer courtesy and of adding value. It is, quite frankly, about the "golden rule" of customer care. Treat the customer as you would like to be treated. Here is one of my favorite examples and all-time pet peeves…

Please Use Other Door.

Picture yourself walking up to the double glass doors of a dental clinic, a retail store, or a building contractor's office. As you approach, you reach out your hand, take the convenient handle on the right (for the large percentage of customers who are right-handed), and you pull or push the door. But, the door doesn't budge because it's locked. Then you see a little sign about waist level that says, "Please use other door." You feel stupid. You pulled the wrong door. You quickly look over your shoulder to see if anybody saw you pull "the wrong door" and fail to see the sign that said, "Please use other door." How could you be so dumb? Do you see what's just happened? As this place of business is about to be blessed by your visit to their offices, they have caused you to feel dumb twice in the process: once for pulling the WRONG door and a second time for not reading the little sign. Now, you reach for the opposite door. It's unlocked and you enter.

I have asked those who manage such buildings why the one door is locked and why it happens to be the door most people reach out to first on their way in to do business. The answer is usually this. "Our security guard unlocks the door from the inside of the building first thing in the morning. He opens the door that is on *his* right facing out of the building. He leaves one door locked because it's easier to lock up again at night." Oh my goodness. Oh my goodness. So, this is about the security guard's convenience. This means that dozens, even hundreds of customers will be inconvenienced all day long so the security guard can open the door easily in the morning and "cruise on out of there" at the end of the day. Is there something wrong with this picture? YES!!! This whole story is so very symbolic and so very important. The symbolism is this: THERE IS NO WRONG DOOR at the front of your offices for your customers. All of your front doors should be unlocked and welcoming to customers. You want it to be so very, very, very easy for people to walk in to do business with you. Please go check your front doors right now.

Friendly, Easy, and Crystal Clear

Another subtle opportunity to smooth the way for customers or to *blow it* big time is with signage and documentation of all kinds. Make it ever so easy for customers to not get lost on the way to doing business with you. Be sure all forms, product instructions, warranties, brochures—all formal customer communication—are simplified yet complete, to-the-point, crystal clear, and cross-referenced to other valuable sources of information that may be needed.

When you answer the telephone, give a complete greeting. Don't say, "Hello, this is Fred." Say, "Hello, Acme Industries...this is Fred speaking. How can I help you?" Any and everything you do to smooth the way signals to customers that you are glad they came...glad they called...and very pleased that they want to learn more about you and your products and your services.

I remember how positively *astonished* I was to visit our neighborhood Bashas' supermarket one day and find a dispenser of hand wipes right at the front door, near the shopping carts. I had read those *Reader's Digest* articles about the ten most germ-infested things you can touch, with restaurant menus and shopping cart handles being near the top of the list. I am a cancer survivor who takes very good care of my immune system. It is very reassuring to take a hand wipe and sanitize the handle of my shopping cart before I stroll around. Someone at Bashas' has smoothed the way for me so that I don't have to bring my own hand wipes or worry about "dirty hands" until I get home to wash them.

What about that pothole out there in your parking lot? Call the strip mall manager right now. Get it patched. One good thump on the front-end suspension of the customer's car sends an unwelcome signal about your place of business. If the folks with the asphalt truck can't come right away, step next door to the ACE Hardware store to get a bag of sand and fill up the hole, temporarily at least.

CWO: Chief WOW Officer

Building on what we learned in Secret #8 about being a Customer-Need-Driven professional, be sure you do everything you do with the customer in mind. As you get ready to hit "send" on an email, sign-off on the installation instructions for a piece of computer hardware, prepare the house for the arrival of its new owners, set up the chairs for your church congregation, stack the cucumbers on a produce stand, or swing the boom on a three-story crane, consider what you do from your customer's point of view. Appoint yourself the CWO, "Chief WOW Officer."

SEAS the Opportunity.

What your customers need you to be is a world-class problem solver. Seize the opportunity. Here's how. First, we spell seize: S-E-A-S. Remember, as you commit to *Smooth the Way* for your customers, some journeys are over the water. There may be rough water and turbulent seas your customer must navigate. Smooth the troubled waters. Be sure there is smooth sailing for your customers.

When a customer brings you a problem to solve or makes a request for service, seize (SEAS) the opportunity: *Summarize, Empathize, Analyze,* and then *Synchronize.*

S – Summarize. Don't *prescribe* a solution until you can *describe* the underlying need. Listen to the customer. Make notes as needed. Be able to tell your client two or three things you've just learned about their situation and get confirmation that you are on the right track. *Example*: If you are an auto mechanic and the customer tells you the car is running rough when they drive over 60 miles per hour, don't say, "Oh, I see. I'll check it out." Say, "So, I understand that the car runs okay at under 60 miles per hour but something is wrong at 60 and above which causes the car to run rough. Is that correct? Is it the engine that's running rough or something about the way the car feels on the road that is rough?"

E – Empathize. Reflect on how the customer must feel about the impact of this situation on his or her business or personal success. How would you feel if you were in the customer's shoes? How would you hope somebody would treat you in such a situation? Thoughtfully acknowledge these customer impacts as you proceed to help. *Example*: If you're selling shoes and the customer says, my shoes always seem to rub on my ankles. Look at the customer and say, "I'm going to find you some shoes that won't hurt your ankles."

A – Analyze. Separate symptoms from causes. Depersonalize the situation so that emotions are put in perspective. Ask for some time to do your homework. Involve the customer in your planning wherever it makes sense. *Example*: If, as a Realtor, you have just taken a home listing and the homeowner is anxious to sell, tell them you will be sure to identify anything that could slow the process down and eliminate these obstacles. The homeowner may say, "I hope you can get some folks to look at our home right away. We can't afford to have it just sitting on the market for very long." By all means, do not take this comment personally. Reply by saying, "I understand. Let me walk through and around your home several times. I'll make a list of what we can do to make your fine home very competitive in the current market." As you share your list, answer their questions. Ask them which items on the list are most feasible for them to address. Work your plan together.

S – Synchronize. Coordinate everything for the customer until a solution is reached. Assure the timeliness of all responses to the customer. Keep everyone informed who needs to be informed. *Example*: If you are preparing to deliver training to your customer's employees, ask for the phone number of the contact person at the hotel where the training will be conducted and for the phone number of the contact person at the company's receiving dock where the training materials will be delivered. Ask for permission to double-check those details that can make or break the professional delivery of your training program. Provide the customer with a copy of your checklist and indicate that you will give them an update when all items are complete. Remember Secret #7 about *taking ownership* and "I am the one." You are the one who will be sure that all the variables work together for a smooth outcome.

Do More...Get More!

There are few industries more competitive than the cell-phone business. A couple of years ago, T-Mobile was experiencing declining customer relations. Customers complained that, when calling with a problem, they got put on hold for "what seemed like eons," and then the customer service reps really weren't much help. T-Mobile was ranked dead last in J.D. Power's customer-satisfaction surveys. T-Mobile's ad slogan had been "Get More." Whoops. The company realized that in their business, customers want their problem resolved fast, in one phone call, and that courtesy matters a great deal. So, T-Mobile revamped the company's hiring, training, and incentive programs. In terms of *smoothing the way* for better service, T-Mobile recognized one huge problem that plagues many companies, which have yet to figure it out. There was a serious disconnect between the marketing department and the customer service department. Marketing was promoting "Get More" while the customer service department was failing the J.D. Power surveys.

As T-Mobile proceeded to change things, they modified their hiring criteria to place far more emphasis on empathy and on quick thinking. They linked everything to a revamped common message and a common theme: "Do More, Get More." The Get More now applies to both customers and employees, while the Do More connects the delivery of service with the marketing promise. J.D. Power has ranked T-Mobile No. 1 for two years running.

Now, besides checking to be sure that both of your front doors are unlocked, call the folks at the local sign company and have them make a medium-sized sign for your front door to replace the one that says, "Please Use Other Door." This sign will read...

Welcome to our place of business.

You are the reason we're here.

Secret #10

Create Options!

There is an important thread of understanding that runs throughout the *Customer Astonishment* training our company provides and throughout this book, in fact. It connects all the key principles and ultimately ties to the *behavior of all behaviors*—a customer-focused behavior that is the single most valuable behavior I can teach. It is both the epitome of your commitment to being a world-class problem solver and, at the same time, the most fundamental thing you can do to *astonish* your customers. It is to ACT or **A-C-T**.

That Funny Little Wall

Come with me now to Home Depot, Lowe's, or your favorite home improvement superstore. Imagine that you own a home that is nearly perfect in many ways and yet it has a few flaws that sometimes annoy you. Chief among these annoyances is the design of the front entryway. The door is off-center on the wall, with the section of the wall to the right being only about three feet wide, which makes it somewhat difficult to decorate.

The year-end holidays are coming and you want the house to be perfect. You would like to do something to that "funny little wall." You decide that perhaps an oblong mirror might be one answer. You drive to the home improvement store. You cross the expansive parking lot, walk through the automatic doors, and begin to search for a sales clerk with that certain-colored apron. As one approaches, you quickly say, "Excuse me; I'm just looking for a mirror."

Switch Roles

Now, put on your carpenter's apron and switch roles. Imagine that you are the home improvement superstore sales clerk and consider the various approaches you could take in serving this customer with his so-called "mirror need."

Scenario Number One: You greet the customer and indicate that the mirrors are on aisle 16. You walk with the customer to aisle 16 and quickly suggest a couple of mirrors that are quite popular. You ask the customer which mirror he likes. He thinks for a minute and then nods at one. (You are happy this process did not take too long as you have other customers waiting.) You help the customer get the mirror down from the display wall. He smiles and walks toward the cashier.

Oops: About an hour and a half later, you are surprised to see the same customer coming toward you. He walks a little faster as he gets near, then stops, looks you in the eye, and says, "I just returned the mirror at the Customer Service desk. My wife hated it. We've got to find something else for the wall." This customer is what we will call the "Rubber Ball Customer." You are playing a guessing game about which mirror his wife will like. He'll keep bouncing back until you get it right or he decides to bounce on over to a competing store nearby.

Scenario Number Two: The heretofore "Rubber Ball" customer now asks you if you have an oblong mirror with an antique gold frame. You say, "No, we don't" and apologize that your store doesn't appear to have the right mirror. You then suggest that he try the furniture store about a mile down the road. The customer leaves.

Scenario Number Three: Instead of saying "No" to the request for an oblong mirror with an antique gold frame, you say, "Yes, I think so. Let me check. Just give me a few minutes." You go to the mirror aisle, check the inventory on the top shelves and realize there is no such mirror. Not wanting to disappoint the customer, you run to the shop at the back of the store. You get some

1x2 lumber, some antique gold wood stain, a piece of glass, and some reflective chrome paint. You begin to make a mirror. Your boss comes by and asks what you're doing. You reply, "I'm just making a mirror for one of our customers." Your boss does not know whether to be amused, congratulate you, or fire you.

Stuck in the Mirror Land of Yes and No

There are two immense problems with what has been going on so far:

(1) You've been stuck in "Mirror Land" attempting to guess which mirror will work when maybe this situation represents something other than just a "mirror need."

(2) You have inadvertently boxed yourself in to having only two options for dealing with your customer: *No, we don't* or *Yes, we do.* In working to *astonish* your customers, the "No" answer is generally uncreative. "Yes," is often the preferred answer, but may represent over-commitment, as your boss was about to point out in Scenario Number Three.

What's the answer? The customer may need something more than a mirror and what the customer needs most is OPTIONS.

Options, Options, Options

Do you recall the three most important things when buying real estate? Answer: *Location, location, location.* Here are the three most important things when working to be a world-class problem solver to create win/win outcomes for your customers: *Options, options, options.*

Let's replay the customer situation above. The customer walks up to you and says, "Excuse me; I'm just looking for a mirror."

Scenario Number Four: You smile and say, "Right this way, our mirrors are on aisle 16." Because you've been here and done this before, you know that *a mirror is not always a mirror is not necessarily a mirror.* As you walk alongside the customer, you politely add to the conversation by saying, "May I ask where this mirror will be used—bedroom, bath, entry way?" The customer replies, "Sure, I've got this funny little wall near the front entry of our house and we've just got to do something creative with it for the holidays."

Mental neon lights flash. Mental sirens sound. Your rich experience is tweaked. You now know that this is not just a "mirror need." In your wisdom as a business person, you now know that you will not be stuck in "Mirror Land." You now know you will not be stuck with just two options with a 50:50 chance you'll be right or wrong. The conversation won't be about "No, we don't have the mirror you want" or "Yes, we have the mirror, thank goodness." It is a "wall decorating need." In your magnificent store, full of so many home improvement wonders, you have a hundred ways to decorate a funny little wall. In fact, to fix the funny little wall there are very dramatic and amazing things you can do, such as tear the whole wall down, move the door to the center of the wall, and install two lovely windows on either side of the door. And, while you're at it you could lay some new 21-inch floor tiles, change the foyer light fixture, and more. Aren't you glad you have so many options for addressing the customer's "fix the funny little wall" problem? Aren't you glad you asked? Aren't you glad you know more than the customer's initial stated "want"? You now know the underlying need is: *to do something creative with the funny little wall.*

So Many Options, So Much Creativity

Now you proceed. If the customer falls in love with a mirror, you're glad you have some mirrors. If not, you mention wall hangings, clocks, changing the wallpaper, and perhaps an elegant floor lamp. If the customer insists on a mirror other than the ones you stock, you tell the customer you have an alliance with the furniture store down the road and would be happy to call them to check on their mirror inventory. Now, you are *expediting*. Congratulations. You didn't abdicate and lose the customer to the furniture store. You are in partnership with the furniture store and still solving the customer's problem. Instead of finding the furniture store to be more resourceful than your store, the customer will always remember that you helped him find the furniture store. Perhaps he'll be back for that small table you showed him that is more affordable than those at the furniture store after all.

And, wonder of wonders, the customer may look at you and say, "You know, I am sick and tired of coming in here at the end of every year to find a new way to redecorate that wall. It is time we remodel the foyer." Eureka, you are about to sell a $4,700 remodeling job. I am willing to bet that 3-5% of the customers who come into Home Depot or Lowe's and say, "I'm just looking for a mirror" end up moving the door and redoing the foyer. Aren't you glad you have…?

* Mirrors,

* Floor lamps,

* Clocks and other wall ornaments,

* Paint and wallpaper,

* An alliance with the furniture store,

* A home remodeling department,

* And other options.

Congratulations, you are a world-class problem solver, giving world-class customer care because you know how to discover true underlying needs and to CREATE OPTIONS for your customers.

To ACT!

So where does A-C-T come in? The next time a customer comes to you with a challenging request and you're tempted to say "No," don't say "No." Next time a customer comes to you with a challenging request and you'd like to say "Yes" and you know you shouldn't, don't say "Yes" yet. What do you do? You ACT!

A – Acknowledge the customer and his/her needs.
C – Circumstances: Discuss these.
T – Tell the customer what you can do.

As you acknowledge the customer, you buy yourself time to think. As you examine the circumstances, you discover underlying needs and also recognize the parameters within which your problem solving will occur. You have not said "NO" and you have not yet said "YES." As you *tell them what you can do*, you show your flexibility AND even a partial solution is better than a roadblock. The message you will send is that you are willing to "work the problem" with the customer. 95% of customers will respond in kind. They will proceed to work with you to find MORE OPTIONS—things you can do in partnership to solve the problem.

To return to our *funny little wall* story one more time: the customer walks in to your home improvement superstore and asks, "Do you have an oblong mirror with an antique gold frame?"

Acknowledge: "Thanks for coming to Lowe's. We have a mirror selection that includes many styles and often there is one that is antique gold. Let's go check aisle 16."

Circumstances: "May I ask where this mirror will be used—bedroom, bath, entry way?" You now learn about the "funny little wall." You arrive at the mirror display to find that there is not an "antique gold" mirror. The customer turns to you and asks, "Do you have any other ideas?" You are not stumped.

Tell What You Can Do: "We can certainly get you the mirror you need, if that turns out to be the best solution for you. However, I can suggest some other things you might do to decorate and change the look of that wall, if you would be interested." Your creativity has been unleashed. Congratulations. You are ACTing as a true business person and not "justa sales clerk."

Put the ACT Principle to Work.

As we conclude this final "Secret," it is important that you are able to apply what you have just learned to your own business situation. You may say, "I don't run a home improvement store with sales clerks." The principle of A-C-T is universal. Let me invite you to do this simple exercise with members of your team.

1. Make a list of the peculiar questions your customers ask, the difficult requests they make, or the challenging situations they somehow create to which you often feel you must reply, "No" or "Sorry, we can't do that."

2. Brainstorm other possible approaches to each of these questions, requests, or challenging situations. Ask yourselves, "What if...?" This is: "What if we could expand the budget and hire some more sales clerks? What if we could rent a piece of equipment for this construction project and do it ourselves without a subcontractor? What if we could create an online course that took two hours instead of having everybody travel to a central site to spend a full day?" Break out of your traditional thinking. Be sure to consider the right partnerships. Ask, "Who could assist us so we don't have to do it all or reinvent the wheel?"

3. Finally, come up with some new answers to the list of questions, requests, and situations in step number one above—answers that are friendly, flexible, and creative. Frame these answers around A-C-T. What are the ways you can *acknowledge* customers and their needs in these situations without giving so-called "knee-jerk" answers that are unfriendly? How can you discuss *circumstances* and not your policies in a way that is informative, shows interest, and is not bureaucratic? What are some alternate or partial solutions that you *can do* where you used to say "No"?

A Message for Owners and Managers

There is one final message. The above illustrations have taken the perspective of a conscientious sales clerk who enjoys working at your store and intends to do right by your customers. The final message is to owners and managers. There is a moment of truth here for you. Be constantly aware of how easy it is to stifle the creativity of an employee who intends to do well. Create a system that recognizes and reinforces all the A-C-T behaviors you want your employees to demonstrate. You could easily stifle the creativity of the employee above. How? Here is a marvelous story that says it all.

I received one of those phone calls nearly all author/consultants appreciate. "We need a keynote speaker to deliver a special message that will uplift our people and support us as we launch a new business development campaign." The call was from a B. Dalton Bookseller executive. He went on to explain that their sales had gone flat and they were looking for any and all new ways to stimulate a return to sales growth.

When the Wind Stops Blowing, Start Rowing.

The company had identified this theme for their employee conferences: *When the wind stops blowing, start rowing.* To propel this theme forward, each employee was given a handsome gold-plated pin with the image of a person in a rowboat, holding oars in each hand. The message of the pin: Each employee is in the B. Dalton boat, the wind has stopped, the sails (sales) have gone limp, and the boat is going nowhere fast. We need each employee to help row the boat.

This is exactly what happened in Flagstaff, Arizona. One young man responded by proposing various OPTIONS for increasing customer traffic to their local store, situated in a stand-alone strip mall. They needed to attract customers away from the big mall, which housed their principal competitor's store. One of the options took into account the unique demographics of the Flagstaff area. It is located in the vicinity of several Indian reservations and is the crossroads for many Native American artists. The exuberant young employee's principal suggestion was to display Native American artifacts throughout the store to make the store more appealing and to create a win/win relationship with the local artists who would be delighted to have their works showcased at a popular retail outlet. The idea worked. People were attracted to the new window displays and found that the inside of the store had taken on more of a mini-museum quality that was much less "commercial." Book sales began to increase. Employee enthusiasm increased. The young man who was the instigator decided to promote the store more aggressively. He designed an inexpensive, but attractive flier and proceeded to place these on the windshields of cars parked at the mall.

Within just minutes, it seemed, there was an angry manager from the mall bookstore on the phone talking to a newly perplexed B. Dalton Bookseller manager, while his now bewildered employee stood by and listened. The angry manager pointed out that the mall was private property and the fliers were placed on cars without authorization. The order was given to the B. Dalton employee to immediately remove all fliers, which he did.

A Sad Day at B. Dalton

It was a sad day at the B. Dalton store. The store was beautiful, sales were up, but morale was way down after this close encounter at the mall. Then, the store staff received word that their regional manager would soon be visiting the store for an inspection. The young man who had been the driving force behind the new store beautification campaign had mixed feelings. He believed the regional manager would like the store, but he just knew he would be hauled on the carpet for messing up the flier thing at the mall.

A Really Big Moment of Truth at B. Dalton

The day of the big visit came. Immediately upon entering the store, the B. Dalton regional manager asked for the young man responsible for the Native American décor. The employee came forward. As he did, he heard the question, "Are you the one who came up with idea?" "Yes sir." "Well, I think the store looks great. About the flier thing at the mall…" "I know, sir, I am so sorry. I didn't mean to mess that up." "Oh, no, you don't understand…" [At this moment, the morale of one young man and that of B. Dalton employees across the country hung in the balance. Depending on what the regional manager said next, the fears of cynics would be confirmed or a belief-building wave would be sent across the company.] The manager continued, "You don't understand. Keep it up. This is the spirit we need. *And, don't worry; we have bail money for creative employees.*" Word did travel like a tidal wave. The "start rowing" message was not just a slogan. Management actually believed the goal they had spoken. They were walking the talk.

As you and your associates ACT in serving and *astonishing* your customers, you will be seen as the creative individuals you are. As you ACT in serving and *astonishing* each other, you will create an enterprise that is *built to last* and built to make a difference.

Conclusion

In the Introduction to the book, I talked about BOLD. What could be more powerful than BOLD? The answer is BOLD Commitment! Do not just read this book and then put it on the shelf. Even if you liked the book and it inspired you, we have all failed. I have failed. The book has failed. And, you have failed. Failed at what? Failed to create a commitment to what you learned in the book.

Have you ever had a million dollar idea? I have. I did not think it was a million dollar idea at the time, but I acted on it and it turned out to be more than a million dollar idea that has sustained my family and me for more than 20 years.

This book contains many million-dollar ideas. As surely as I know I am typing on my Dell computer on this Thursday afternoon as I complete this book, I know, of the thousands who will read this book, there will be MANY who find the million dollar ideas contained in it. Be one of them. They will change something about their companies or their approaches to their careers that will translate into a million dollars of incremental business revenue or lifetime income. It is my mission to help you prosper. As you prosper, you will be happier and you will do more good in the world through your generosity.

So, which million-dollar idea in this book did you miss? Read the book again. As a minimum, browse its contents and summarize several BIG IDEAS that can be your own "tipping points" for leadership in business and success in life. And, once you decide on your big ideas, make a commitment. Make a BOLD Commitment to ACT on what you have learned. Make *Customer Astonishment* who you are.

Epilogue
Sort This Out!

As I was doing a final reading of my own book, I was also reading the amazing book by Thomas Friedman, *The World is Flat*. It makes me ponder a huge dichotomy: Are we in an age when "customer care" truly matters or in an age when this concept is slowly being replaced by an automated, technology-driven, Web-based answer for everything? Are we willing to forego the human touch just to get whatever we need faster and cheaper online? Thomas Friedman constantly challenges his readers to "sort this out"—to make sense of the information age, globalism, and the traditional ways of doing business we have been accustomed to. As I work to "sort it out," I recall a very recent customer service experience of my own that may guide us to find the balance between *high-tech* and *high-touch*.

Tipping Point: Laryngitis

Last weekend, my wintertime encounter with the common cold turned into what a professional speaker / author dreads most: laryngitis. One of my local clients is using my talents repeatedly to address groups of 25-30 people and I have been "dumb enough" to let myself lead these long meetings without the aid of a good microphone. I have sometimes hooked up my old $99 Radio Shack unit with minimal benefit. I finally decided that this must end. I must protect my precious vocal cords. I would upgrade to a professional, portable, personal PA system. I was overdue. I certainly deserved one. And, I had to find one quickly before my next voice-box-threatening meeting.

Radio Shack doesn't sell a high-end unit at their stores nor does Circuit City. So, I picked up the yellow pages and telephoned several professional audio-visual stores in the Phoenix area. I tried three. There were three common answers to my inquiry about PA systems as given by uniformly sleepy-sounding sales clerks at 4:30 in the afternoon, as their stores were getting ready to close:

- "Ahh-uhhh, what is it you want? Oh, yeah, we can get stuff like that."

- "No, we don't have any here at our store."

- "We can contact some vendors like LiteSpeed or Anchor or Sender to see if they'll ship one for you. It'll take a couple of days to get it here."

Save Me!

Okay, end of "live customer care" scenario. It was a disaster. So, I turned to the new flat world (read flat panel display) attached to my Dell computer. (That flat panel display is very symbolic of the *flat world* Mr. Friedman talks about.) I went to Internet Explorer to Google to enter "portable PA sound systems" in the browser window. There I found dozens of confusing Websites, but I resonated to a friendly one called www.seeoursound.com. I clicked. The SeeOurSound folks were obviously an online outlet for several manufacturers. They had the Anchor brand displayed. I clicked. I quickly found the AN-130 Basic Package for $515. Small, portable, right price (the guy on the phone at one of the stores had told me to expect to pay as much as $700 to $1000). I decided to call the 866 phone number on the screen. I got Bob Lorincz on the line. He's the chief technical guru, Website designer, owner, and sales manager for SeeOurSound. He's a multi-business, homegrown, all-American entrepreneur based in Wagoner, Oklahoma. He knew his stuff. He took my credit card info and ordered me an AN-130 unit from the manufacturer's warehouse in Los Angeles to be shipped to me via UPS, two-day air, in time for my next long meeting with 30 people the following Friday.

The Message

What's the major message here? Please consider reading Thomas Friedman's book and Tom Peter's book, *Re-Imagine*. Be afraid. Be very afraid, and then get over it. The message is that you can't plan on doing business the way you've always done it. Bob Lorincz of SeeOurSound represents the *flat world*. I have to believe that at least two of the three *round-world*, audio-visual systems stores I called in Phoenix will be out of business sometime in the future. Who needs the storefront, the yellow pages, or a not-too-savvy sales clerk who doesn't have any local inventory to show me anyway? Besides, I suspect such a sales clerk may also end up going to the Internet.

Alas, Customer Care?

So, where is customer care in all this? I had turned to the local stores via the yellow pages to get some up-close-and-personal customer care—to see, touch, and feel the merchandise in a real store. It didn't work. What I really wanted and needed most was to just get a suitable PA system at a good price, fast. The Internet and Bob Lorincz saved me frustration, a trip across town, and considerable time. Bob could have even been less than chummy and got my order as long as he could tell me it was a quality unit and would be here in two days. Now, lest we despair in our commitment to personalized customer care, here is the delightful human punch line. Bob was very friendly. He was both knowledgeable and Oklahoma friendly and he was not encumbered by a lot of overhead items other retailers often trip over. Here was the *flat world* for me: A knowledgeable, friendly man talking by phone as I looked at his catalog online while he prepared to place my order and process my payment with the amazing electronic tools at his fingertips. He brought a customer in Phoenix together with an audio-systems guru in Oklahoma, together with a manufacturer's warehouse in LA, together with an air courier and all with the click of a few buttons and a few minutes of conversation over the phone. Problem solved. Customer satisfied. And, "customer care" was nevertheless evident in Bob's patient, friendly manner. His use of technology to expedite the solution was his power. His "customer care" was the competitive edge that will reduce the likelihood that I'll peek at his competitors' Websites. His Website may even end up on my Internet Explorer "List of Favorites."

The Brave New World

We must learn and love the technology. We must learn from Bob Lorincz. We must see the convergence of all this on the new *level playing field* of the one, shared world we have created for ourselves. You see, I now know where to instantly get the entire scoop on portable PA systems and I've got a friend in Wagoner, Oklahoma, who can get me one. That's a tough combination for the old-line, *round-world* Phoenix audio-visual systems retailers to beat. We cannot hide behind the sales counter, behind our storefronts and apologize that we have nothing in stock. If you happen to have a store, that's fine, but act like you don't unless the customer really needs to visit one. If you don't have a store, the world is flat. Go for it. And, in either case, be alert and friendly to your customers.

Customer Astonishment is about progress, about using all the latest technology tools to expedite solutions to your customers' problems. And, *Customer Astonishment* is always about how much you care that they (the customers) found you—in the yellow pages, at your store, or at your Website. They found you. Your gratitude will be evident in those subtle ways you add that human touch wherever you possibly can. *A computer can do the work of 50 ordinary men and women. No computer can do the work of a single extraordinary man or woman.* You are extraordinary. Your customers will be positively astonished by the *total* solution you and your team represent.

Recommended Books

Leverage: How to Create Your Own "Tipping Points" in Business and in Life, Darby Checketts

9 Lies That Are Holding Your Business Back: And the Truth that Will Set It Free, Steve Chandler and Sam Beckford

The Small Business Millionaire, Steve Chandler and Sam Beckford

Re-Imagine: Business Excellence in a Disruptive Age, Tom Peters

Execution: The Discipline of Getting Things Done, Larry Bossidy and Ram Charan

The Tipping Point: How Little Things Can Make a Big Difference, Malcolm Gladwell

Customers for Life: How to Turn that One-Time Buyer into a Lifetime Customer, Carl Sewell and Paul B. Brown

The World Is Flat: A Brief History of the Twenty-First Century, Thomas L. Friedman

Built to Last, James Collins and Jerry Porras

100 Ways to Motivate Others, Steve Chandler

The Joy of Selling, Steve Chandler

Ten Commitments to Your Success, Steve Chandler

Ten Commitments to Networking, Larry James

Appendix
Additional Friendly Tips for Astonishing Your Customers

A) From Darby's journey across the USA in search of American Pride, including interviews with hundreds of American workers…

The Top 4 *Pride Killers*…Get creative to get beyond these.
1. "Monotonous work" (Practice "job enrichment.")
2. "Lack of future goals for me" (Avoid the "dead end.")
3. "An intimidating boss" (Genuinely listen to employees.)
4. "Bureaucracy" (Streamline forms. Explain WHY procedures matter.)

The Top 6 *Pride Builders*…Put these to work.
1. To perform against known *standards of excellence* and to triumph
2. To receive the honest praise of others
3. To own, use, or create things of beauty, value, precision, and dependability
4. To uphold values and traditions
5. To finish a task and experience the feeling of "doneness" (completion)
6. To experience a sense of contribution

B) Things "Active Listeners" Do

1. Don't talk (so much).

2. Avoid *trigger words* that unnecessarily create negative emotion and defensiveness: words that assign blame or imply an unwillingness to help, which are somehow cynical, overly critical, or sarcastic.

3. Show signs of life (nod your head; give a friendly grunt of approval as you listen).

4. Choose helpful questions. Know the difference between questions that *show interest* and those that put the speaker *on trial*. ("Could you please tell me more about that last detail?" versus "Why did you say that?")

5. Manage distractions. (Go to a "place" where you can listen and pay attention.)

6. Find the value in what the speaker is saying, even if you don't like the speaker.

7. Check for understanding through paraphrasing. (Rephrase and repeat what you heard.)

8. Accept responsibility for misunderstandings. (Instead of, "You weren't listening," say, "I may not have said that well. Let me try again.")

C) How to Sound GREAT on the telephone

G – Greeting…Give one that is complete. (Roll out the red carpet.)

R – Resonance…Speak slower and lower your voice at the end of some sentences.

E – Enthus-i-a-s-m…Last four letters = I Am Sold Myself. (Or, use call forwarding.)

A – Articulation…Remember the consonants and gently accentuate these.

T – Technique…As you put on hold or transfer, avoid losing the customer in the *Phone Zone*.

D) If you're feeling all stressed out, use the practical concept of S-M-P-O-B. (Remember it as: "Send Mail to the Post Office Box and don't internalize it.")

S	Self	Know what you believe, what you do well, and what is truly important.
M	Mind	Read. Talk briefly with someone who'll listen. Laugh now and then.
P	Perspective	Remember: More things generally go well than don't.
O	Others	Choose not to compare. Reserve judgment. Serve and *astonish* them.
B	Body	Breathe freely. Walk briskly. Eat the good-for-you stuff.

E) Handling Difficult Situations

In General...

1. **Be agreeable.** If you can't agree in fact, then agree *in principle* or agree *provisionally*. For example, a customer says, "That invoice is incorrect." If it is, apologize for the error and get it fixed. If it is not, say, "If there's an error in that invoice, I agree we need to fix it. Let me double check for you."

2. **Be steadfast.** Don't allow the customer to be abusive or to violate standards of ethics, safety, and product quality. Calmly escalate the situation to your boss.

3. **Deal with issues, not personalities.** Fix the problem, not the blame.

4. **Let the customer finish his/her story without interrupting.**

5. **Deal with specifics, not generalities.** If the customer says, "This is a stupid product design," don't argue. Ask the customer, "So that I can assist you, please tell me what it is about this product that you don't like?"

6. **Take a break to buy some time.** Ask the customer if you can take a minute to check things out and get back to them. As you do, they'll cool down and you'll have time to get creative.

In Conversation…

1. **Let the person finish the thought or worry he/she is trying to express.**

2. **Depersonalize the situation *in your mind.*** (It's NOT about YOU!)

3. **Objectively acknowledge the person's frustration.** Say, "I can see that this procedure is causing some frustration."

4. **Paraphrase the problem as a goal.** Say, "Let me take a look at the procedure to find a way to make it easier to follow." (There is always a way.)

5. **Buy some time.** (See the list above).

6. **Agree in fact or in principle with whatever he/she says next.** Even if they say, "You're too slow," respond with, "If this procedure appears too slow, let me see what I can do to speed it up a little."

Even if you can't agree, *be agreeable*. This is customer care, *not* customer war. And, remember: ***Oh blessed are the flexible, for they shall not get bent out of shape.***

About the Author
Darby Checketts

Darby grew up on a small ranch in South Phoenix, Arizona, where his family raised quarter horses, sheep, turkeys, watermelons, and dates. He and Sharon are the parents of seven fantastic children: Natalie, Vance, Denise, Cheryl, Ken, Brent, and Matt. Darby and Sharon live in Mesa, Arizona, where they manage the activities of Cornerstone Professional Development, which they founded in 1985. Together with their various partners, they expound the principles of *Customer Astonishment* and *Leverage*. Darby is president of the company and also serves as its principal trainer and strategist. He has worked with hundreds of organizations, large and small, around the globe. Literally millions of individuals have benefited, directly and indirectly, from his in-person teachings, his books, and various other publications. His professional career began with Ford Motor Company and includes experience with several other companies where he served in a variety of management and professional positions. He has traveled throughout 47 of the 50 United States and 25 countries on five continents. Darby's first loves are God, family, and country…followed by his love of supporting his clients as they achieve their goals, and by opportunities for community service and travel. **Customer Astonishment** is Darby's seventh book. His most recent books are…

Leverage: How to Create Your Own Tipping Points in Business and in Life

Dancing in Peanut Butter: A Guide for Handling "the Stuff that Happens" in Life

Please visit www.DarbyChecketts.com. Telephone Darby at 866-654-0811.